TT IN CAMERA

COURSE MILESTONES

Parliament Sq
May Hill and Cruickshank Car
Milntown
24
23
Waterworks
22 Hairpin
Lezayre
Gooseneck
Glentramman
25
21 Glen Duff
Sulby Bridge
Kenrowmoar
20 Ginger Hall
26
Guthrie Memorial
Sulby Straight
19 Sulby Crossroads
27
18 Quarry Bends
Mountain Mile
Ballacrye Bend
28
17 Ballaugh Bridge
Mountain Box
Stonebreaker's Hut
Alpine Cottage
29
16
Bishopscourt
Veraniah
Rhencullen
30
Birkin's Bends
Graham Memorial
15
Bungalow 31 Hailwood Rise
KIRK·MICHAEL
Douglas Road Corner
Brandywell
14 Cronk Urleigh
32
13
Bottom of Barregarrow
Windy Corner
Barregarrow Crossroads
33
12
Keppel Gate 34 Creg-ny-Baa
Handley's Corner
Kate's Cottage
LITTLE LONDON
Drinkwater's Bend
Gob ny Geay 35
11
Brandish Corner
Cronk-y-Voddy
Hillberry
Lambfell
Cronk ny Mona 36
10 Cregwillys Hill
Signpost Corner
Sarah's Cottage
Glen Helen
Bedstead Corner
37
Governor's Bridge
9 Laurel Bank
Doran's Bend
START
Bailig
Bray Hill
8 Ballacraine
1
Ballaspur
Greeba Bridge
Appledene
Greeba Castle
The Highlander
Crosby
Glen Vine
Union Mills
Braddan Bridge
Quarter Bridge
7
6
5
4
3
2

THE COURSE

GLEN HELEN
LAUREL BANK
KIRK MICHAEL
BALLAUGH BRIDGE
BALLIG BRIDGE
BALLACRAINE
BUNGALOW
SULBY BRIDGE
CROSBY
RAMSEY HAIR PIN
CREG NA BAA
EAST MOUNTAIN GATE
START
UNION MILLS
KIPPEL GATE
B
GOOSE NECK
QR. BRIDGE
GOV. BRIDGE

There is no such thing as a map naming every Isle of Man TT vantage point partly because, with seemingly over a thousand bends flowing into each other, there just isn't room, even on the Landranger Area 95 Ordnance Survey map. Most of the names are not towns or villages anyway, but rather pubs or cottages associated with TT circuit marshals over the years, or of individual course milestones. Others have been named because some famous rider died or came to grief there.

The TT course maps featured here are the ones used by the race authorities, either in their programmes or on the start-line scoreboard, and indicating signalling points. Nowhere on them, though, will you find the likes of Ago's Leap, which lies just beyond the bottom of Bray Hill, or Snugborough, just before Union Mills, or the infamous 'Black Dub'; nor will you find Whitegates or Stella Maris, both in Ramsey, early on in the climb up to the Hairpin. The Nook is a decidedly nasty right-hander on the drop between Bedstead and Governor's Bridge, and Governor's Dip follows the latter and leads into the start/finish straight. Incidentally, named points often evolve: Barregarrow on the Ordnance Survey map but Barregarroo on the course, while Birkin's Bend is now better known as Rhencullen.

TT
IN CAMERA

A photographic celebration of the
world's greatest motorcycle road races

Don Morley
Foreword by Geoff Duke OBE

First published in May 2007

A catalogue record for this book is available from the British Library

ISBN 978 1 84425 419 4

Library of Congress catalog card no. 2007921999

Published by Haynes Publishing,
Sparkford, Yeovil, Somerset BA22 7JJ, UK.
Tel: 01963 442030 Fax: 01963 440001
Int. tel: +44 1963 442030
Int. fax: +44 1963 440001
E-mail: sales@haynes.co.uk
Website: www.haynes.co.uk

Haynes North America Inc., 861 Lawrence Drive,
Newbury Park, California 91320, USA.

Printed and bound in Great Britain by
J. H. Haynes & Co. Ltd, Sparkford,
Yeovil, Somerset BA22 7JJ

Picture credits

All photographs were taken by Don Morley, other than two pictures of himself – the action shot on page 14 (top), which was kindly loaned by Malcolm Wheeler of Mortons Motorcycle Media Ltd, and the portrait on page 15, which was loaned by John Watterson of Isle of Man Newspapers.

Thanks also to Getty Images, who now own the copyright of some of Don Morley's earlier work – including the images on pages 23 (bottom), 32 (top), 40/41, 58 (bottom), 60 (bottom left and right), 77 (bottom) and 78 (bottom) – and to MCN/EMAP who likewise own the copyright of the two photographs of Agostini on page 37.

CONTENTS

To Don,

Thank you for this and all the other superb photos which help to remind me of the glorious 1950s and the TT. Superb photography, and thanks for the memories.

Geoff Duke OBE
Six-times World Champion

BELOW Geoff Duke, before the 1953 races, still with a Norton helmet rather than that of his new team, Gilera.

RIGHT Geoff Duke, surely the greatest all-round racer ever, seen here on the Mountain climb en route to winning the 1955 Senior with his works 500cc four-cylinder Italian Gilera.

Press photographers did not have the benefit of rangefinders or through-the-lens viewing screens on their cameras in those days, so we carried a tape measure instead, then watched and memorised the various top riders' practice lines very carefully, marking these precise spots by pressing something like a tiny blob of Plasticine or silver paper into the road surface. The next job was to measure the distance from that point back to where we intended to stand during the race – and I might add of 'the Maestro', Geoff Duke, that he alone hit my marker on every one of the 1955 Senior's seven laps, despite extreme heat causing many other riders to slide about on molten tar.

Duke was inch perfect and, more importantly, phenomenally fast; indeed, the race's timekeepers credited him with having covered his third lap in 22m 39s, meaning the first-ever 100mph lap had been achieved at long last. The roars of approval from the fans could be heard all over the Island; many had been anticipating the elusive ton lap for over a decade. Almost everyone wanted it to be achieved by Geoff, a universally popular Lancashire lad. Imagine our horror when we learned later that the official timekeepers had decided to round his speed down to 99.97mph – a terrible, and highly controversial, travesty given that they were only using hand-held clockwork stopwatches in those pre-digital days! Sadly, Geoff had also been robbed of overall victory by a similarly bad official decision the previous year, although the man himself was far too much of a gentleman ever to complain. Believe me, everyone else did.

L ife changed forever for me on 6 June 1953. It was just after dawn had broken, at about 4.45 on a rather cold, damp morning, and a new motorcycling friend and I were standing shivering at the top of Bray Hill on the famous Isle of Man TT course. The memories of that day would remain forever engraved on my mind.

Despite that morning's cold, and having travelled all through the night to get there, our excitement was still intense for we were actually quite close to the race's start line. We'd already seen the red Very light warning flare go off and light up the sky, so we knew practice for the 500cc Grand Prix World Championship-counting Senior TT race was about to begin. Moments later virtually every one of that era's road racing greats thundered past at near touching distance, with the likes of us just standing on the adjacent pavement watching for free as all our heroes raced away over the Island's absolutely unique 37.73-mile public road course. For me, this amazingly long and varied circuit, which passes through villages and towns in addition to climbing its way right over a mountain, has always been mind blowing – and not least because of the course's proximity to the spectators. It is, in fact, even more so today with the vastly faster modern

LEFT The author as a young man, just back from covering the 1972 Olympics and festooned with Nikon cameras. The big Novoflex 400mm telephoto lens, looking a bit like a gun, occasionally got me into big trouble, especially when I was covering wars: the soldiers' adage 'Shoot first and ask questions later!' was a regular jibe.

BELOW My 51 years' worth of TT programmes and 47 years of accumulated TT course press passes, plus a couple of the little flags issued once your bike had had its petrol tank pumped out for the sea crossing. I used to leave my flags fixed to the handlebars all year round, like badges of honour, so most eventually disintegrated. These two are all I have left.

The crash helmet is the one I wore from 1953 onwards. I raced in it many times, and still wear it today if out taking pictures with a bike. Why? Well not because I haven't got a better one! This style, unlike the modern jobs, allows me to get the camera up to my eye and shoot pictures without taking the helmet off, gaining the vital seconds that have won me many extra TT shots over the years while dashing, against the clock, around various vantage points.

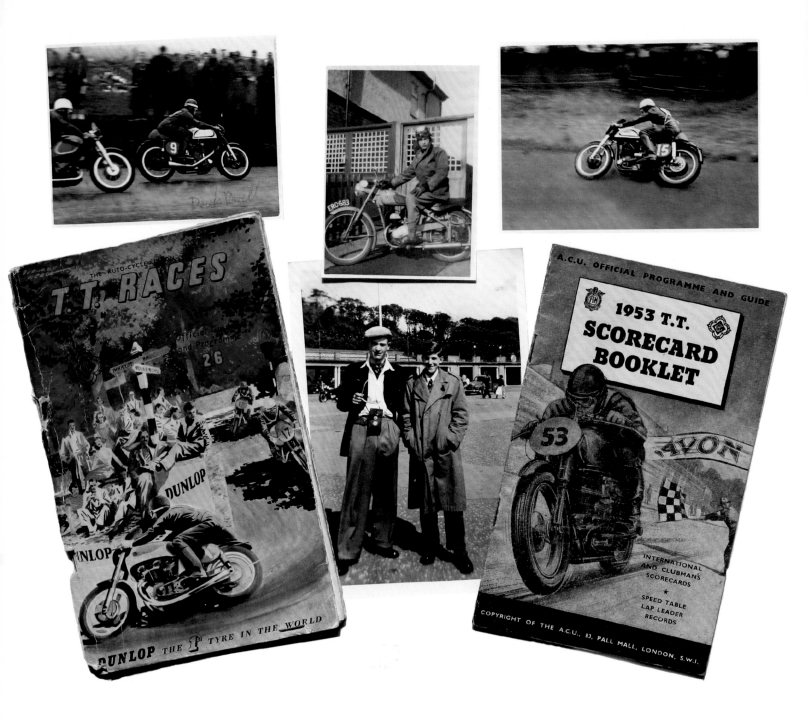

Memorabilia from 1953

The TT race programme, scorecard and some of my earliest photographs.

TOP LEFT *Derek (D. T.) Powell, on the Norton, and Bob McIntyre on one of the last outings for the exotic AJS 'Porcupine', a bike whose engine was designed before the war and intended for supercharging.*

TOP CENTRE *The author about to set off for the Island from home in Mickleover, Derby, on his little 125cc Francis Barnett pop-pop. Liverpool and Mona's wonderful isle were a long way away with a bike whose top speed was a mere 48mph!*

TOP RIGHT *John Surtees was drafted into Norton's 1953 TT works team as a replacement for the injured John Storr. He was very nearly kicked out again by the autocratic team-manager, Joe Craig, after John crashed and injured himself on another make of machine in the Lightweight race, putting him out of the more important Senior TT. Craig was furious by all accounts, but could not help but recognise John's very obvious incredible talent. He kept him on Norton's books for the future – and, of course, the rest is history for this multiple World Champion.*

CENTRE *The author with camera case and new-found friend Geoff Rice, photographed on Douglas seafront across the way from the Villa Marina, where all TT prizegiving took place. As hinted, the camera was not in its case, but set up on a nearby wall to take this picture via the delayed action setting.*

Memorabilia from 1954

TOP LEFT The only picture ever taken of Geoff Duke's ill-fated pit stop in the 1954 Senior race. The race had been delayed several times, then eventually started in what most agreed were totally unacceptable wet, windy and dangerous conditions, and with visibility down to just 50 yards on the Mountain. Sadly, one rider died before the stewards decided to review the situation but, rather than stopping the race, they reduced the overall distance from seven laps to four – all unbeknown to the long-suffering riders already racing out there. Race leader Duke pitted for petrol and fresh goggles, but the equally oblivious second-placed Ray Amm was carrying extra fuel so his Norton carried on. Then, to the Gilera pit crew's horror, came the announcement that the stewards were shortening the race. There is little doubt Duke would also have carried on – and won – as his Gilera still had more than enough petrol for another lap. Worse still, it had taken so long to come to a decision that by the time the race ended the entire Island was bathed in sunshine! It wasn't Amm's fault, of course, and it was a hollow victory, but Geoff Duke had been robbed of the race win, as he would be denied that 100mph lap at the following year's TT.

TOP CENTRE Australian Gordon Laing pushes his outside flywheel works Norton off to start at that same ill-fated Senior. Gordon had only just been drafted into the works squad and did brilliantly to finish sixth. Sadly, he was killed at the Belgian GP later that season.

TOP RIGHT Ray Amm pushes off to start – and win – the 1954 Senior on the Joe Craig-designed 'Proboscis'. We did not know then it was to be the last of this brilliant engineer and Norton team-manager's unique works bikes.

CENTRE There was nothing more exotic, and no team management more slick, than the German 125cc and 250cc works NSU set-up. They even had massive engine warming machines by the start line, then changed the oil for boiling oil just before the flag dropped so their riders could race flat out immediately; other riders' machines would need a mile or two to warm up. Hans Baltisberger is seen here on the NSU 250 racer – and if you think the bike looks familiar it probably is! The virtually all-conquering NSU team pulled out of racing a year or two later and sold their bike designs and tooling to a tiny company called Honda, as yet unheard of outside Japan.

I had been signed to work exclusively for the weekly newspaper Motor Cycle News *for 1957, and as* MCN *then came out a day earlier than either of the other two specialist weeklies it meant deadlines were horrendously tight. My top priority was literally to snatch a picture of George Salt pushing off his 350cc Norton to start the Junior TT, which was the opening race of the week, then run to where my 1000cc Vincent motorcycle was parked ready to ride like a lunatic to the offices of the* Isle of Man Examiner *newspaper who had agreed to let me use their darkroom facilities. The idea was I should process my film, then dash off again at breakneck speed to the tiny little Manx airport at Ronaldsway to meet an amateur pilot who would fly it back to the mainland in a 1930s 'Tiger Moth' bi-plane. All wonderful in theory, but it soon went horribly wrong, for the newspaper office was closed for the bank holiday, and we didn't have a Plan B, so I then dashed round to Douglas's rival paper, praying they'd be open and amenable. Fortunately, bended knees weren't called for, but I knew the plane couldn't wait and there was no time left for niceties like washing or drying the film, so I just tied the processed but very wet and sticky roll of film onto my Vincent's handlebars, and hoped it would still be there – and dry – by the time I got to the airport. We made the front page of the issue by the skin of our teeth, also beating the opposition by a full day.*

machines and far quicker lap times. Experiencing pure road racing from such incredibly close quarters really has to be seen to be believed.

On that first morning my new companion and I were comparative strangers. We had both ridden up through much of middle England to catch the midnight ferry from Liverpool to the Island, where the first actual words spoken between us were of our mutual shock at discovering the shipping line was insisting on draining our motorcycle fuel tanks of petrol before sailing. For two young innocents such as us this was a disaster. Petrol was still rationed after the war, but not knowing of this policy we had both filled up our bikes quite close to the docks: we had thus wasted not merely our money and all the petrol, but also most of our precious ration coupons. Now we would have to rely on public transport rather than our beloved bikes to get about on the Island. The shocks didn't end there, either, for although our first crossing was moonlit and smooth, it was also decidedly eerie because our little vessel was forced to spend so much of its time slowly picking its way between the numerous bombed, mined or torpedoed merchant ships still jutting up out of the water as ghosts from the Second World War. Indeed, it would take many more years before all of these numerous wrecks were cleared.

Our next concern on docking in Douglas involved watching the motorcycles being unloaded while swinging back and forth as they were winched off, ten or twelve at a time, by a crane. Fortunately no damage was done. However, as ours were virtually without petrol we decided simply to dump them both by the quayside, and we then set off on foot for TT practice and the top of Bray Hill.

It was as though heaven had opened up for us soon after we arrived there, as umpteen Italian MV Agustas, Gileras and Moto Guzzi multis went thundering past, followed by many works AJS, Matchless and Norton motorcycles and even a very special BMW factory racing twin. These were all machines that we would have no hope whatsoever of seeing on the mainland, for at the time the TT was the UK's only road racing World Championship event.

The first man past was the hugely popular Englishman Les Graham, on a 500cc MV Agusta, followed by a rival four-cylinder Gilera four piloted by the Valentino Rossi of his day, the immortal Geoff Duke. Apart from being a brilliant trials rider and a top-level car racer, Geoff was also the multi 350 and 500cc road racing World Champion, internationally known then as 'the Maestro', after being so dubbed by the sport-loving Italians.

Fergus Anderson followed on a futuristic in-line, rather than across-the-frame, four-cylinder Moto Guzzi employing aircraft rather than motorcycle technology for its almost fuselage-style main space frame. This exotic machine also utilised very unusual experimental full streamlining which had been constructed by stretching a thin layer of magnesium foil over a flimsy, almost crinoline-like, outer framework. Anderson's works Guzzi was also known to be good for over 170mph, no mean speed in those days on that era's ultra-skinny, pre-radial construction tyres, but all was not well with it that morning as Fergus flashed over the top of the hill to start his second practice

lap. The wind pressure had obviously been getting under the fairing contraption and, at that moment, was literally ripping it to shreds.

Fergus never even backed off the throttle, but fortunately I managed to grab a slightly less than sharp picture of it flashing past, showing great shards of magnesium foil trailing behind like multitudinous kite tails. This particular shot was used later in several magazines, and was thus my very first scoop, but sadly it can't be shown here as it has gone missing over the many intervening years. Anderson failed to come past again – he must have been forced to pull in and retire somewhere – and the Moto Guzzi mechanics then fitted a far more conventional and secure fairing to this machine for the race. However, in taking and selling that one single picture I had taken my own first steps away from my job in engineering towards a brand-new photographic career.

I had taken my entire £5 personal fortune to the Island to pay for everything, including food, petrol and lodgings, and had fortunately spent rather more of it than perhaps I should on buying just two rolls of 120 sized black and white film to use in my, even then, very old 1930s folding camera. This, of course, was used to take most of the earliest pictures reproduced here. For much the same seriously cash-strapped reasons I negotiated a decidedly cut-priced boarding house deal which involved my sleeping in a bath rather than having the use of a bedroom. I cared little about such minor discomforts, as they were worth it just to be there, though I would now have to admit to being a lot less keen about having to get up in the night whenever anyone else needed to use *my* little bathroom!

Surprisingly, my new-found acquaintance, Geoff Rice, eventually decided motorcycle racing wasn't for him, and our paths never crossed again after that week. Much sadder still, the great Les Graham, who had been the first rider past us on Bray Hill, tragically crashed and died there in the Senior TT race itself, just yards away from where Geoff and I had been standing. He had already smashed the race and lap records whilst winning the Ultra Lightweight race a day earlier and his untimely death came as a terrible shock to us all. Even worse to recall, Les was the first on a now very long list of names of riders who, during my own career, have similarly lost their lives while racing in this otherwise so beautiful Island. Many of those who died later I counted as personal friends.

Tragic as the TT race statistics undoubtedly are, however, I still take great comfort from the fact that they all chose to be road racers but then died doing what they loved best. My eldest son was named after my good friend, Gary Hocking, a double TT winner who was also the reigning double world motorcycle racing champion before switching to cars. Gary changed to four wheels because he felt it might just prove to be a bit safer in the long run, but then tragically lost his life almost first time out in a race car. While mentioning sons, my youngest also has a TT connection, being born during June 1965 while Mike Hailwood and Giacomo Agostini were battling it out on 500cc MVs in the Senior event. Both of them eventually crashed out, but Mike was able to remount and go on to win – and no prizes for guessing where my son's impending dad was, as you will see from my pictures in the book! These were taken by that time, incidentally,

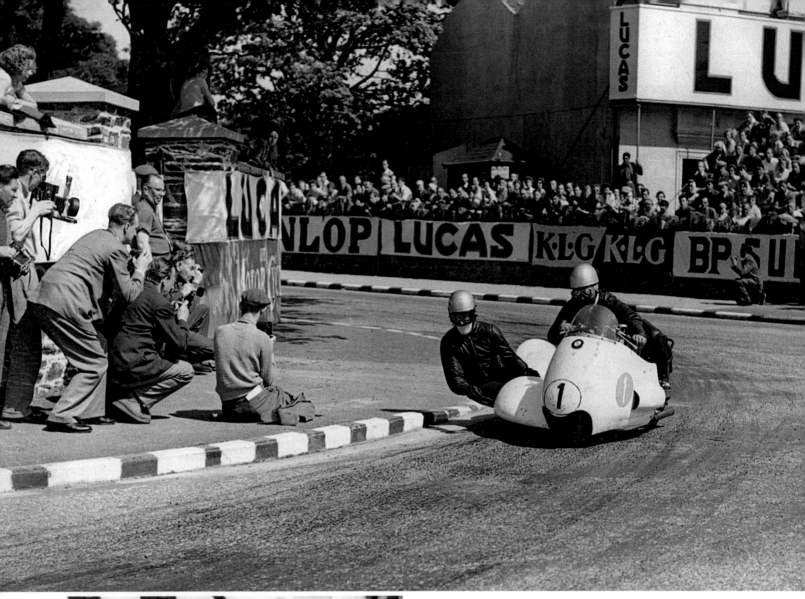

ABOVE *Walter Schneider with passenger Hans Strauss on the shorter Clypse circuit en route to record lap and race speeds with a works-entered 500cc BMW during the 1958 World Championship-counting International Sidecar TT. They are at Parkfield corner, at the top of Bray Hill, where the Clypse circuit used to turn right off the full TT course a mere couple of hundred yards or so from the start line. The kneeling press photographer (with cap on) amidst this gaggle is the author with his Speed Graphic plate camera.*

LEFT *The same corner as above, but taken a few moments later on that Speed Graphic, from the pavement, and of course from my side of the track, and featuring the then former World Sidecar Champion Eric Oliver and a certain Mrs Pat Wise. I was waiting for this shot because, although retired, Eric had bet someone he could still achieve a top-ten placing even if he rode an ordinary road-going outfit with conventional separate sidecar, and used a member of the public as passenger (who, incidentally, would have to sit there like the proverbial tailor's dummy rather than climb about to balance it like a racing partner). Amazingly, the authorities allowed him to try. Even more amazingly he actually pulled it off, with tenth place on an ordinary Norton 'Dominator 88' 500cc road bike with a Watsonian 'Monaco' sidecar fitted, and won valuable World Championship points into the bargain. We never saw anything like that again!*

with the 35mm Leica rangefinder-type camera which replaced my various older Agfa and Rolleiflex roll film cameras, and even my larger plate format, ex-WWII Speed Graphic.

While talking about photography, I should mention that TT spectators and amateur photographers alike can stand or sit at least as close to the action as I can which, unlike at any other major circuit, truly does mean *very* close. The bad news for photographers at the TT, however, is that there are far fewer picture opportunities per race, due to the extreme length of the Island's 37.73-mile circuit. Some TT classes have as few as three laps, for example, and so to increase the number and variety of picture angles we professionals spend rather a lot of our time dashing back and forth between different vantage points during the race – usually via the Island's many minor back roads, or even green lanes – in the hope of being able to catch and re-photograph the top riders several times on each lap. This always requires fine timing plus several pre-race-day rehearsals, and it helps to have the use of a good, fast, lightweight motorcycle rather than a car, for many of the Island's better picture viewpoints are virtually inaccessible to four-wheelers.

Modern digital cameras and wireless picture-sending technology, on the other hand, have eased many of our other photographic operating problems. We no longer have to spend hours working inside blacked-out hotel wardrobes to develop our films, for instance, because we don't even use film any more. Nor, for the same reasons, do we need to rush to get our filmed results to the nearest airport to meet deadlines, for digital photography is virtually instant, producing pictures that can be sent worldwide from the side of the track within seconds by mobile phone and a laptop computer.

Personally I would not have missed a single moment of doing things the hard way, not least as it was all those hard-learned experiences and TT lessons which ultimately opened so many other doors, and led to my long enjoying near non-stop world travel while photographing numerous other great subjects. I have taken pictures of whatever was happening at the time at the United Nations, and covered several small wars. Add in numerous Olympics, five World Cup soccer tournaments (England 1966 included), and many more two- and four-wheel Grands Prix to a royal wedding or three, plus Winston Churchill's state funeral, dozens of world title boxing matches and countless major international tennis, golf or athletics meets, and all the one-to-one photo shoots with most of my era's greatest stage and movie stars, and that is indeed why I still feel so privileged.

Come TT fortnight, however, there really could be only one place in the world you might find me, and I still owe this unique event, the riders and, of course, so many of the Manx people themselves a very considerable debt of gratitude for so much kindness and help over the years. Special mention must be made of that wonderful band of unpaid, volunteer TT marshals who do such a difficult, dangerous and sometimes distressing job with so much dignity and skill, whatever the weather.

My thanks likewise to the great Geoff Duke who, though he never knew it, truly motivated my photography, and my own long-running competitive motorcycling career, and who has also now done me the great honour of writing a Foreword for this book. Thanks also to broadcaster, Manx GP chief press officer and former TT chief press officer Geoff Cannell, whom I have long regarded as being 'Mr TT'.

Thanks also to the publishers, Haynes, and most especially to editorial director Mark Hughes for actually having the idea of my doing this book and then, much more so, for his enormous help and support, and to Kay Edge for knocking my scribbles into shape. Finally, I must say a very big thank you to my dear wife Jo, who is a very fine TT and Grand Prix photographer in her own right, but who so often sacrificed her career interests for mine (and, what's more, has always kept me in tea!).

BELOW Formality has never been one of my strong points, which is why I always declined invitations to the annual Isle of Man Governor's reception. Wild horses wouldn't get me into a suit, even when I was invited again in 2003. Eventually, TT chief press officer Geoff Cannell said, very pointedly: 'Look you have just got to go.' Although feeling very out of place in casual gear I am so glad I did, for His Excellency the Lieutenant Governor of the Isle of Man, Air Marshal Ian Macfadyen, CB OBE, announced he was going to make 'a very special presentation'. Like everyone else I craned forward to see what it was all about, and was amazed and almost moved to tears to hear my name being called out, and to be presented with this wonderful award as recognition of my 50 years of journalistic contribution to the TT races. My thanks must also go to photographer John Maddrell and sports editor John Watterson of the Isle of Man Examiner newspaper who were not only present but apparently in on the secret. They sent me this picture from what was, as it turned out, my last but one TT week.

1950s & 1960s

A GOLDEN ERA

This was a golden period, for not only did it encompass 1957, the TT's own Golden Jubilee year, but the Island also showcased the mega talents of numerous legendary riders, including 1950s stars Geoff Duke, John Surtees, Ray Amm, Werner Haas, Rupert Hollaus, Carlo Ubbiali, Luigi Taveri, Bill Lomas, Fergus Anderson, Dario Ambrosini, Cecil Sandford, Les Graham, Tarquino Provini, Bob McIntyre and many others. By the 1960s the rider talent pool expanded to include more immortals like Mike Hailwood, Phil Read and Giacomo Agostini. Many of these racers had umpteen world titles apiece – those were special days indeed.

It was an amazing technological era, too. Relatively small and unsponsored companies, like Moto Guzzi for instance, were able to produce incredibly exotic race machines like the famous 500cc water-cooled V-eight. The Japanese countered later with Swiss-watchlike engineering and physically tiny machines, employing anything up to six-cylinder engines with twelve- or fourteen-speed gearboxes. Indeed, during part of this period Honda were racing a minute 125cc bike with five cylinders and twelve speeds.

In the later 1960s Honda's wonderful little six-cylinder 250cc was opened out to 297cc, so as to make it eligible also for the 350cc class. They did the same thing with their equally small and stunning four-cylinder 250s, although this formula of 'stretching' failed them in the 500cc class as the chassis failed to cope with that much extra power.

Nothing much has challenged the engineering specifications of those truly great TT and GP machines since, but even they didn't win everything. AJS, Norton and Matchless also fielded very successful works teams, as indeed did BMW and NSU. However, all these were frequently topped by magnificent Italian motorcycles from the likes of MV Agusta, Gilera, Moto Guzzi, Mondial, Aermacchi, Ducati, Benelli and Moto Morini. Put this into a modern context and, since the TT lost its World Championship status, we now get excited if even one major manufacturer sends over a solitary 'works job', whereas then there were dozens from umpteen different rival factories.

It was not all good news. Professional UK TT photography, at least, still remained in the dark ages, with colour action pictures virtually unheard of. Mostly this was due to the era's newspaper and magazine publishers demanding we continue using old-fashioned, large-format plate cameras. Luckily, however, a few of us went out and bought our own 35mm Leicas, hence the early colour pictures in this book!

This sums up the best of the 1950s and 1960s: glorious weather and crowds all the way up and over the Mountain. Here at Keppel Gate they're watching Norton privateer aces Tom Thorp (leading) and Brian Setchell battling it out for personal bests in the 1961 Senior. Neither would win, not least as a certain Mike Hailwood was victorious in this and two other TT races that year, but both finished in the top 15. Each would have received a small silver replica of the Senior TT "Winged Mercury" trophy. The precise formula for awarding replicas has changed over the years but, as a generalisation, the first 20% of starters to finish win a silver, and the next 15% win a bronze. Tom and his wife now live on the Island, and Mrs Thorp is currently Honorary Secretary of the TT Riders' Association.

LEFT The immortal Geoff Duke posing for me. A former telephone engineer and Royal Signals despatch rider, Geoff burst into prominence as an amateur rider in 1949 when he pulverised the opposition while winning the 500cc Clubman's Senior TT. A few months later he achieved another record-breaking Senior win at the Manx GP. In fact, he very nearly scored a Manx double that year, taking a decidedly close second place in the 350cc Junior race. Hardly surprisingly, he was then snapped up by Joe Craig to go professional as a fully fledged member of the works Norton team. Duke went on to win another six International TTs plus two second places and a fourth, en route to winning his six world titles. (It could so easily have been seven; he missed out by a single point one year after a tyre-shredding incident.)

RIGHT By 1953 'the Maestro' had switched from Norton to the Italian Gilera concern. They were only running a 500cc class bike, effectively ending Geoff's chances of winning any more 350cc races or world titles, but he is seen here as the reigning 500cc World Champion, about to weigh the big Gilera in for the 1955 Senior TT. The compulsory 'weigh-in' was (and still is) a leftover term from when motorcycle sport followed horse racing's format. Bikes and riders were weighed before each race for handicapping purposes. Prior to handing the bike in, Geoff would have wheeled the Gilera past a long line of seated 'trade barons' asking him to confirm which make of oil, petrol, tyres, magneto, spark plugs, carburettors and chains his machine was using. The trade paid big bonuses to whoever won while using their products in return for being able to advertise their TT success. Geoff and Gilera should have done rather well out of them that year, for not only did he win the following day's Senior event, he also smashed the 1955 race and lap records.

BELOW Double TT winner John Hartle at the same weigh-in, with one of the very last outside flywheel works 500cc Nortons from the Joe Craig era. This is one of the rarest of race bikes, but a lot scruffier in its era than those seen in mint condition in museums today. Indeed, the battle scars on John's 'works' bike were probably collected over more than one season.

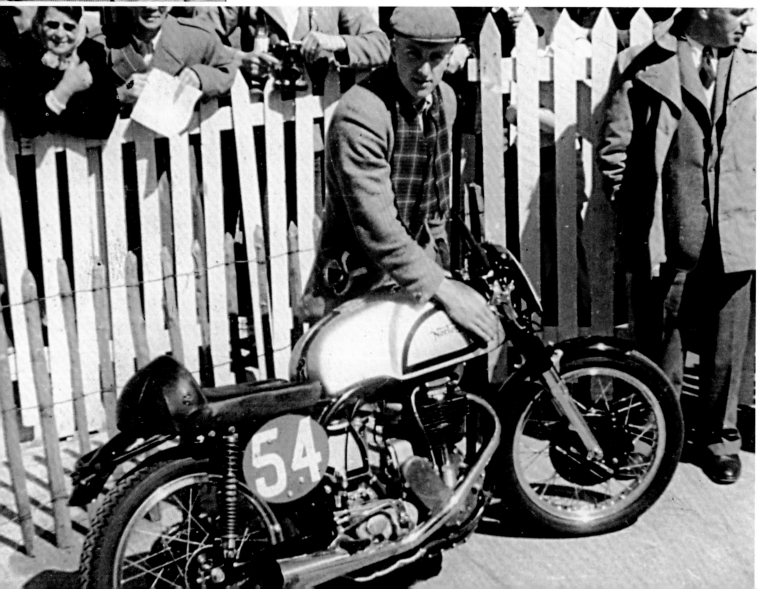

TOP LEFT Double winner and multiple World Champion W. A. 'Bill' Lomas winning the 1955 Junior race on the 350cc works Moto Guzzi at Brandish, a view unchanged in 99 years, but which would be very different for 2007 after the bulldozers moved in.

BOTTOM LEFT Another multi TT winner and World Champion, Gary Hocking of Rhodesia, seen at Parliament Square and winning again in 1960 on the 350cc four-cylinder MV Agusta. A good friend (my eldest son was named after him), he was killed later in final practice for an F1 car race.

ABOVE Geoff Duke came out of retirement on a one-off basis in 1959 to ride this 350cc Duke/Reynold's Norton special in the Junior TT, taking fourth place and acquitting himself well against the latest stars and their much more exotic machinery.

ABOVE The famous 1957 Moto Guzzi V-eight, unquestionably the most exotic water-cooled 500cc GP race machine ever built. What's more, this is almost certainly the only period colour picture ever taken of it, with R. H 'Dickie' Dale on board at Creg-ny-Baa during that year's Golden Jubilee Senior TT. This semi-prototype bike was phenomenally fast in a straight line when running on all eight cylinders but, due mostly to magneto problems, this didn't happen often and it then became a pig to ride, with various cylinders chiming in, or out again, at different times. Moto Guzzi's boffins ran out of time to get it sorted because they, and most other works teams, pulled out of the sport later that year, quoting the unacceptable cost of racing. Thus the wonderful V-eight sadly never reached its potential, although Dale did finish fourth on it in this race.

LEFT Jack Brett exits the Governor's Bridge dip during the 1957 Senior on his – by then – hopelessly outclassed single cylinder factory-entered 500cc Norton.

ABOVE RIGHT Bob McIntyre, in perfect racing conditions at Creg-ny-Baa, en route to the first ever 100mph lap and victory in the Golden Jubilee Senior TT, riding the injured Geoff Duke's four-cylinder Gilera. Undoubtedly a truly great and gifted rider, Bob unfortunately had the ability to be rather too fast for most of his bikes: he often shattered lap records prior to blowing up his overstressed engines. Although long dominant in many TT races he only won three, including this 1957 Junior/Senior Gilera double.

RIGHT McIntyre kicked off the eight-lap Golden Jubilee Senior with a new record of 99.99mph – and this, we should remember, was from a standing start – then he smashed it again with 101.03mph on his first flying lap. He topped this amazing feat on lap four with a staggering 101.12mph, but perhaps fortunately then backed off at the behest of his decidedly worried signallers. Bob had not only broken the 100mph barrier at long last, he also set a new average race speed of 98.99mph. Here he is on lap four, blasting the streamliner down Bray Hill. (Full streamlining was banned from all circuits a year later after a spate of accidents involving riders being blown off course.)

LEFT It might seem obvious, but championships are won by winning races rather than smashing lap records, and John Surtees was perhaps the finest exponent of winning, and by the necessary safe margin. Here he is being congratulated immediately after crossing the finish line to win the 1958 Senior on the four-cylinder 500cc MV Agusta. To the left is his team-mate, John Hartle (in a mackintosh), and in the centre could that be the great Italian mechanic, later team-manager, Arturo Magni?

ABOVE Surtees won the 1958 Senior at 98.63mph, with a best lap speed of 100.58mph. This is in 1960 at Governor's Bridge, making fresh TT history by becoming the first rider to win three Senior TTs in a row. John won that race at 102.44mph and then, with John Hartle and Mike Hailwood breathing down his neck, pushed the 500cc lap record up to 104.08mph. This was the last of this brilliant multiple World Champion's TT wins, for he then switched to car racing, making history again as the only person ever to win crowns on both two wheels and in Formula 1.

RIGHT The remains of John Hartle's Senior bike, 1958. Poor John had to leap off his MV at near full speed when the fire he didn't even know was raging reached his wedding tackle. The precious machine was left to burn out mere yards from the start/finish line and, believe it or not, there wasn't a single fire extinguisher in sight!

ABOVE Mike Hailwood blasts his 125cc Desmo Ducati off the start line en route to a third-place finish in the 1959 125cc Ultra Lightweight race, one of the few massed-start solo TTs. Mike made TT history by winning four silver replicas in a week.

LEFT By now largely retired, Geoff Duke had a much less happy time that week while trying to master the quirky handling of his works 500cc BMW.

ABOVE RIGHT Walter Schneider and Hans Strauss by the Manx Arms at Onchan on the Clypse circuit, well on their way to winning the 1959 International Sidecar TT. Note the people in house doorways and the press photographers on the pavement with plate cameras: no one could hope to get much closer.

RIGHT A rare view of Bob McIntyre winning the 1959 Formula 1 TT race on the Joe Potts-entered 500cc single cylinder Norton. This was a new race class, but one the motorcycle manufacturers and trade argued against so strongly that it was never repeated. The picture is also rare because of the bird's eye angle, achieved by standing high on top of the parapet of Governor's Bridge, which was allowed then but certainly not now.

OVERLEAF This 1960 Senior TT start shot illustrates rather well how things used to be – the big stars have long since started, the truly exotic works machines have all gone too, so now at last it's the turn of the supporting cast. A gaggle of no-hoper road-going BSA Gold Stars, or similar single overhead cam International Nortons rather than Manxes are now waiting their turn to shine, or possibly even convince someone they are the stars of the future. The flag-bearing Boy Scouts are stoically still standing as honour guards, by now with mighty tired arms.

LEFT Carlo Ubbiali swoops down to Hillberry from Brandish on the late 1950s 125cc double overhead cam MV Agusta. Carlo won five TTs and finished second seven times.

ABOVE Former Moto Guzzi and Norton works rider Ken Kavanagh at Braddan on the 500cc Norton.

RIGHT Mike Hailwood rounding Creg-ny-Baa on the 'Privat' MV Agusta during his epic 1962 Senior TT battle with team-mate Gary Hocking. On that occasion Hocking won after Hailwood's bike suffered clutch failure – much to the delight, incidentally, of even Mike's British fans, who objected to the use of that 'Privat' badge. MV were pretending they had merely lent Hocking and Hailwood the bikes and that it wasn't a proper works-backed effort, which fooled no-one. The Italian company were supposed to have withdrawn in 1957, alongside great rivals Gilera, whereas they actually continued racing without any effective opposition, the decidedly exotic works special 350 and 500cc MV Agustas dominating everything. Every other rider had to go for standard, over-the-counter British production machines, so the real race for the fans was not about the winner but who would come third.

ABOVE The 1961 250cc Lightweight TT was perhaps the greatest race ever. Japanese manufacturers Honda were at their absolute peak, so the outcome was predictable, but Bob McIntyre was not in the official GP squad and had been lent a spare four-cylinder works bike by the company's UK importers with the proviso that he wasn't to win! To a man like 'Bob Mac' this was the proverbial red rag to a bull: he immediately showed his true colours by shattering every known record, blitzing to a 98.83mph lap from the standing start, then on lap two upping the record again to just 0.042s short of the magic ton. Two more shattering laps of 99.26 and 99.13mph put McIntyre literally miles ahead of Honda's works GP squad, Mike Hailwood, Tom Phillis, Jim Redman and Naomi Taniguchi; Bob was actually lapping by this stage at 5.4s a lap faster than John Surtees's 350cc record. It could not last, though, and McIntyre gave the thumbs-down signal as he passed the pits to start the final lap 34s in front of Hailwood. We had no doubt Honda's top brass were breathing great sighs of relief at that signal, and again when the news came that our hero was out of the race, retiring at Quarry Bends with a seized engine, but we were all terribly sad the dream ended that way. Even we had to acknowledge, though, that had Bob won he would have taken vital World Championship points away from Honda's regular works team riders. Needless to say, he was never again lent a works Honda, and was tragically killed at Oulton Park a year later when his machine aquaplaned during a horribly wet UK race meeting. Geoff Duke was moved to write that 'we have just lost the best road racer of all' – quite an accolade – although, given that racers also have to win consistently, my view is that both Geoff himself and John Surtees were better riders.

BELOW LEFT Hugh Anderson of New Zealand was another great all-round road racer who always knew exactly what he had to do. Seen here flat out on Bray Hill during the 1961 Junior on a 350cc single cylinder AJS. Anderson finished seventh on that occasion but went on to win two TTs and become a multiple World Champion.

RIGHT Billy McCosh at Quarter Bridge, well on his way to a very fine sixth place with this scruffy-looking G50 Matchless during the decidedly mixed weather of the 1965 Senior race.

BELOW Mike Hailwood crashed the 500cc MV during a phenomenal dice with Giacomo Agostini in the 1965 Senior. He suffered little more than a bloodied nose, though the big MV's fairing and windscreen were smashed, a footrest broken off and one exhaust pipe so badly flattened that Mike knew if he could get it going again this normally four-cylinder machine would be unlikely to run on more than three. He managed to kick most things straight and set off, but by then Agostini had also crashed in the wet, at exactly the same place as Mike, leaving the British rider to wobble round in the mostly awful conditions to another fairytale win. The fastest lap of this ding-dong was a mere 95.11mph, slower than John Surtees's effort seven years before.

The Island's stone walls can be seriously bad for one's health, as 'Ken' Takahashi found out when he hit one full on with his works 125cc Honda at Union Mills in the 1962 Ultra Lightweight race. The popular little Japanese rider had led every practice session, putting in several fastest laps prior to this incident.

LEFT Dave Croxford at Quarter Bridge in Douglas, heading for eleventh place with his G50 Matchless in the 1965 Senior. Despite his hard-earned nickname of 'Crasher', Croxford was a consistent performer who went on to win a Production TT.

ABOVE Giacomo Agostini made his Senior TT debut in that same race, as Mike Hailwood's partner in the MV Agusta team. It wasn't a dream debut for 'Ago', as he universally became known, because he slid off in the wet at Sarah's Cottage.

RIGHT By 1967's Diamond Jubilee races he was on a new and much easier to ride three-cylinder machine, and fast becoming *the* man to beat.

LEFT Selwyn Griffiths with both wheels clear of the deck, flat out down Bray Hill on his Matchless G50 during the 1965 Senior, when he came fifth. He never quite won a TT, and neither has his son Jason yet, but they have four Manx Grand Prix victories between them.

BELOW Mike Hailwood at Ramsey Hairpin in the 1967 Junior race with the incredible six-cylinder 297cc Honda. Mike never contested the Manx but he won 14 TTs, more than anyone in history until Joey Dunlop came along.

ABOVE Kel Carruthers pushes his 250cc Benelli off for the 1969 Lightweight race alongside the Kawasaki of Dave Simmonds, winner of that year's 125cc Ultra Lightweight. Carruthers won this race with an average speed of 95.5mph and a new fastest lap of 99.01mph. He went on to become the 250cc World Champion for Benelli in 1969.

RIGHT 'Siggi' Schauzu and passenger Hans Schneider made the Sidecar TT their own during the 1960s and early 1970s, winning an amazing nine times. Here they're seen on their victorious 500cc BMW outfit at Creg-ny-Baa in 1969.

1970s

FALL AND RISE

The TT continued as a full Grand Prix event well into the 1970s, but by that time it was in serious crisis. Few top riders or works teams wanted to race on the Island, mostly because of the staggering cost of competing there compared to other GPs. All the other World Championship-counting races in those days were run on mainland Europe so, unlike the TT, did not require complicated travel arrangements and expensive ferry crossings. To make matters worse, TT practice and racing took a full fortnight, whereas all the other GPs were over in three to four days. The Belgian round, for example, began on a Thursday afternoon with unofficial practice and there were timed sessions on the Friday and Saturday. All six GP class races took place on the Sunday, and then everyone left for the next race or enjoyed a relaxed drive home. TT qualifying took a week by itself, and could only happen just after dawn or near to dusk when the Island's roads were closed. This left the riders fretting for the rest of the day, unable to get on with the difficult job of learning the race lines round this ultra-dangerous and demanding 37.73-mile road course.

Another worrying difference was that it has always proved impossible for TT riders to be given a warm-up or sighting lap. This has meant that even the more inexperienced among them have to race flat out from cold on the start flag, despite this unique circuit being lined with stone walls and mountain drops compared to the other GPs catch fences or run-offs. By this period, too, many riders were getting killed or seriously injured on the Island and, hardly surprisingly, an increasingly powerful lobby was demanding the TT either be banned or at least dropped from the World Championship calendar, which did happen after a top rider boycott led by Phil Read and Giacomo Agostini.

Devoid of both status and international stars, the TT then declined into something of a home-rider backwater. Happily things picked up again later in the decade when the sport's ruling body threw the TT a lifeline by giving the production machine-based Formula 750 class world status after renaming it the 'TT Formula 1' class for 1977 onwards. Phil Read ended his personal boycott and, somewhat controversially, won both this race and the 1977 Senior while also earning himself his eighth and final world title. Although Read's return wasn't seen as a particularly good omen by some, no-one complained a year later when he went head to head with Hailwood on Mike's own fairytale return from retirement. Between them, they arguably saved the world's greatest road races, and brought tens of thousands of spectators back to the Island.

Things had also greatly improved photographically by then. There had been some terrific advances in the design of 35mm cameras, including the invention of motor drives, and lenses were vastly improved, especially from manufacturers like Olympus and Canon.

The 1970s were lean times after virtually all the GP stars decided to boycott the TT on safety grounds. The event also lost its World Championship status. Indeed this looked like the beginning of the end – or it did until 1978, when a certain long-retired rider and ex Formula 1 driver decided to come over from New Zealand to have a holiday and what he described as "a bit of fun and just one more wobble round". Stanley Michael Bailey Hailwood's magical return is history now, as is the fact that the fans came back in droves to watch him. There was hardly a dry eye when Mike and his Ducati flashed across the finish line to win the F1 race, not least as he had beaten his old adversary Phil Read. But now the Island was full of spectators again, and the TT's future seemed assured.

LEFT Alex George negotiates
Bray Hill on the works
Triumph triple he shared with
Dave Croxford to win the 1975
750cc Production race.

ABOVE Helmut Dahne, at
Creg-ny-Baa in 1974, is racing
to third place in the 1000cc
Production race with his
BMW R90S.

RIGHT Another great TT
protagonist, and nowadays
commentator, 350cc Yamaha-
mounted Charlie Williams
finishes second to Mick Grant
in the 1977 Classic TT race.
Charlie was a particularly
versatile rider who, apart from
world endurance racing and
many mainland honours, very
deservedly won nine TTs. The
1970s was a confusing and
difficult period for the Island's
races: with World
Championship status just
about lost, the authorities
tried many differing race
formulas in a desperate
attempt to give the now
seriously ailing TT a lifeline.

TOP LEFT The 'Barrow Boys', as the sidecar lads and lasses are fondly known, always fully supported the Island's races, and none more so than multiple World Champion Rolf Steinhausen with passenger Josef Huber, seen here in 1976 on the start line pushing their 500cc Konig outfit away just ahead of George O'Dell and Kenny Arthur.

LEFT Steinhausen and Huber won in 1976 from Dick Greasley with Chris Holland, and Mac Hobson with Mick Burns.

ABOVE Another great TT and GP pairing, Trevor Ireson and Clive Pollington, at Ramsey's Parliament Square, well on the way to winning both Sidecar races in 1979.

LEFT A mid-1970s Junior TT start shot, complete with traditional boy scouts and flags, and a massive array of talent waiting to go, including Tony Rutter (6) and Chas Mortimer (5), who won eight TTs apiece. Alex George (7) won three, as did Tom Herron, who is in the green, white and red leathers in the background. Steve Tonkin (4) won just once.

ABOVE AND RIGHT Among members of the TT's great supporting cast in this era were Manxman Kenny Harrison, seen here with sparks flying from his F3 bike as he grounds it down hard at Ballacraine, and Malcolm 'Mal' Lucas on full song with the BeeBee brothers 250cc Yamaha at the Bungalow railway crossing.

LEFT Tony Rutter, father of current star Michael, having overtaken Manxman Kenny Morrison on Bungalow Bends and momentarily leading the 1976 Lightweight race. It wasn't to be Tony's day on this occasion however: the eight-times TT winner eventually slipped back to fourth.

TOP An all-Yamaha Junior 1–2–3 in 1976. Congratulating each other are Chas Mortimer (centre), the winner, third-placed Billy Guthrie on the left, and Tony Rutter, second – and just look at the dead flies covering the front of Rutter's bike!

ABOVE The word 'immortal' is probably used rather too often, yet who could deny this description of 'Ago', the popular Italian racer with the film star looks or, to address him properly, Giacomo Agostini. From playing second fiddle at MV to Mike Hailwood this phenomenal rider truly came into his own at the 1968 races with a Junior–Senior double, and fastest laps in both. Then, as if to underline his superiority, Ago repeated this feat in both 1969 and 1970. Six wins and six fastest laps in a row were unprecedented successes, although the downside was that the Junior and Senior TTs began to look like one-horse races. That's probably why many spectators cheered when Agostini's usually ultra-reliable MV broke down on the first lap of the 1971 Junior race.

RIGHT Ago won the 1971 Senior with yet another fastest lap though, and in 1972 it was back to normal, with him scoring his last-ever double double. Following Gilberto Parlotti's death in the Ultra Lightweight race, however, both Agostini and team-mate Phil Read vowed they would never compete at such a dangerous circuit again.

The loneliness of the long distance runner! Rolf Steinhausen and Josef Huber had taken over from Siggi Schauzu and made the International 500cc Sidecar race their own by the mid-1970s, winning three TTs. As here, with their Konig outfit flat out on the ultra-bumpy Cronk-y-Voddy straight, they were often miles in the lead.

LEFT My old friend Mick Grant, at the Gooseneck, winning the 1978 Classic TT on the 750cc 'Green Meanie' Kawasaki and the first rider to average over 110mph. Mick was arguably the last of the genuinely all-round road racers, a World Championship GP winner as well as a TT ace who could ride just as well on the short circuits and mix it with anyone. Grant almost single-handedly kept the bigger capacity TT classes alive after the withdrawal of Agostini and so many other GP stars, winning seven TTs and notching up countless fastest laps.

ABOVE A canny Yorkshireman, Mick always claimed fastest laps didn't count for much. He also claimed never to have actually raced in a TT because that was far too dangerous – although he conceded he could tour round rather quickly, as illustrated by the amount of daylight between Ballaugh Bridge and his GP-winning works 250cc Kawasaki! He is now a brilliant engineer and trials rider.

Two interesting period pictures taken in the late 1970s from the same vantage point, just below Creg-ny-Baa – or perhaps we should say from above! For one year only the TT authorities built a temporary bridge so fans could cross the course during the races. Photographically, of course, this was a heaven-sent opportunity to get a different view. The rider in the picture on the left is John Jones, on a 250cc McVeigh Yamaha; I can't tell who the one on the right was, but if you look at the very furthest point of road you will also see a couple of other riders just about entering Brandish Corner, an ultra-fast left-hander named after Walter Brandish, one of the TT's earliest casualties. Neither Brandish nor this view had altered throughout the TT's history, but at the time of writing the bulldozers were moving in and Brandish, at least, was due to look totally different for 2007 and the 100th anniversary year. The Island's traditional grass-covered stone walls were to be flattened here to provide the next generation of riders with a modicum of run-off, but experience suggests this will merely tempt some to take this still very dangerous bend that little bit faster.

The brilliant Pat Hennen, seen at Braddan Bridge (below) and then Ballaugh (left), in 1978. The American looked on course to beat his works Suzuki team-mate, Barry Sheene, and also Yamaha's Kenny Roberts, to win the 1978 500cc Grand Prix Championship – until this fateful Senior TT race. Pat had taken a new lap record with a speed of 113.83mph while battling for the lead with Tom Herron on the previous lap, then tragedy struck. Just minutes after this picture was taken, Hennen was hit full in the face by a large bird, mid-way through the remote and ultra-fast Bishopcourt section, crashing heavily. He was critically injured, with head injuries so severe that he spent most of the following year in a UK neurological unit. Happily he recovered well enough to lead a near-normal life, but the crash ended an extremely promising racing career.

ABOVE Takazumi Katayama won the 1977 350cc GP World Championship title as a Yamaha privateer and, like Pat Hennen, came over to the Island to have a go at the TT in 1978. The first to arrive at the scene moments after Hennen's crash, and discovering Pat's motionless body amid the wreckage, Katayama made him as comfortable as possible, then ran up the road to warn other riders. His great presence of mind probably saved Hennen's life and prevented further accidents. Of course it also cost him his own top placing (and not inconsiderable prize money), and so it gave me much pleasure, as one of the judges, to nominate Katayama afterwards for the International Valour in Sport Award. Shortly afterwards I had a very secretive approach from Honda in Japan, who confided that they were about to come back into GP racing and would I suggest who they should consider as riders. My choices were Katayama, who always seems to be referred to as Japanese though he was actually a Korean living in Japan, and another equally pleasurable nomination: Mick Grant.

RIGHT A mirrored image I rather like of TT fans watching Irishman and arch enthusiast Courtney Junk racing through Ballaugh, in a late 1970s Senior race.

LEFT Bill Smith won four TT races and more finishers' replicas than anyone in the event's history – and this famous Chester motorcycle dealer must also have sponsored more riders than most.

BELOW LEFT Grand Prix star Tom Herron usually rode works Yamahas or Suzukis, but he's seen here on a privately entered Mocheck Honda, at Douglas Road corner just entering Kirk Michael village, during the 1978 F1 race. Tom won three TTs but failed to figure on this occasion.

BELOW RIGHT John Williams long held the accolade of being the fastest though not the luckiest man on the Island, despite winning the Classic and Production races twice. Here he's swooping down Bray Hill on the works F1 Honda, en route to placing second to Mike Hailwood in 1978.

RIGHT Alex George, climbing the Mountain at the Guthrie Memorial, was Honda's big white hope for the 1979 F1 title, and he won fairly easily from Charlie Williams and Ron Haslam after the battery came adrift on Hailwood's Ducati, dropping him down to fifth.

LEFT Phil Read made a comeback at the 1977 races after vowing, along with Agostini, that he would never ride a TT again. In fairness, Phil had felt the circuit was far too dangerous for World Championship status, obliging (or even pressurising) riders to compete there against their own wishes when vital points were at stake. He took a lot of stick on his return, especially from vociferous Manx people who reckoned his principles had been influenced by the large pot of gold then on offer. Phil felt there was no reason not to race now there was no obligation, and he announced that he was riding for his own enjoyment rather than the money. This brilliant but often controversial star is seen here at Ballaugh Bridge en route to winning the Senior TT again, on his privately entered 500cc Suzuki.

ABOVE Rider number 2, pushing off with Read in 1978, is the great Joey Dunlop, someone we shall certainly be seeing more of later.

RIGHT Read, riding for Honda, on the last lap at Governor's Bridge. He won his eighth TT (and final world title) in the one-off World Championship-counting F1 race in 1977.

LEFT The man himself, Mike Hailwood, with the Steve Wynne-prepared works F1 Ducati on the start line in 1978 – and looking very apprehensive. Few knew that Mike had earlier crashed another bike during a final practice session for the Junior race, almost ending his fairytale comeback before it began.

ABOVE No worries. "Mike the Bike" has a laugh on the 1979 start line, more than 20 years after his phenomenal racing career began. In 1973, during a spell as a Formula 1 driver, he was awarded the George Medal for bravery after twice diving into a blazing inferno to save the life of Ferrari driver Clay Regazzoni. A year later Mike suffered a massive crash himself and was invalided out of F1 with a right leg so badly damaged that the bones had to be virtually fused together. Theoretically this made motorcycle braking or gear changing nigh on impossible although, judging by his fantastic 1978/9 TT performances, it would seem no one had actually explained that to this superman!

RIGHT Pub signs on the course exhorted the legendary Mike the Bike to win that F1 race – and he did, by two minutes and with a fastest lap of 110.6mph. There was the added satisfaction of passing his old adversary, Phil Read, before the latter's works Honda decided to quit.

ABOVE There was great rejoicing as Hailwood flashed over the 1978 F1 finish line – and an awful lot of sore heads the next morning, the great man included, after the champagne started flowing (left). Why not, at such a magical moment: none of us would ever see anything like it again!

ABOVE RIGHT And what about the Junior race, and that Yamaha 250 which had thrown Hailwood off in practice? Well it was actually a bit of a dog, and the best our hero could manage was finishing in a rather distant 12th.

RIGHT The following year Mike was back again, this time with a 500c Suzuki and a new supposedly 'works' Ducati for the F1 race, which soon began falling to bits. He did very well indeed to nurse that home to fifth place – but by then another fairytale was unfolding. It's strange how everyone in motorcycling remembers Hailwood winning his comeback race, yet few seem to recall that in 1979 he also rode a two-stroke RG500 Suzuki to a stunning victory over the established stars in the Senior race. Indeed, this supposed 'holiday racer', seen here at Braddan Bridge, smashed both the race and lap records with a 111.75mph race average and a record fastest lap of 114.02mph. Equally forgotten is that he very nearly repeated this success a few days later, in the 1000cc Classic TT, where he missed victory by just 3.4s to Alex George and the works Honda. It would prove to be Mike's swansong race.

One of the most popular innovations of the very late 1970s was letting a few carefully-chosen past masters back on the closed-road TT course. The great pre- and post-war German racer, Georg 'Schorch' Meier (above) was able to demonstrate he'd lost little of his prowess while riding the works supercharged 500cc BMW on which he'd won the 1939 Senior race. Similarly, Freddie Frith (above left), the former 350cc World Champion and four-times TT winner, went out on his former ex-works KTT Velocette, now lovingly restored by Ivan Rhodes, seen pushing him off. Luigi Taveri (left), the great post-war Swiss Grand Prix star and triple TT winner, hardly looked a day older or slower on the ex-works Honda 125cc four.

ABOVE Ballacraine, and the Irish toffee-maker Stanley Woods who had ten TT wins before retiring at the start of the Second World War. For this 'past masters' event he came back to the Island on crutches, needing two hip replacements, and had to be lifted onto his old Velocette. Amazingly, Stanley then lapped at nearly the same speed as his best time on the bike, when he won the 1939 Junior race – what a hero!

LEFT Double TT winner and multiple World Champion Bill Lomas later demonstrated the incredible Moto Guzzi V8, and is seen with it here in the company of fellow TT and trials riding ace Sammy Miller.

RIGHT The immortal Geoff Duke on one of his early 1950s 500cc works Nortons, showing he'd lost none of his natural ability, or wonderful riding style, with nothing whatsoever sticking out!

OVERLEAF A favourite shot to conclude the 1970s, simply showing a whole gaggle of sidecar lads and lasses traversing the short semi-straight between Quarter Bridge and Braddan Bridge.

1980s

ON A FRESH CHARGE

Confidence in the TT's future was back, not least as international offshore banking had taken over as the Island's main money-spinner, relieving much of the previous pressure on the races to bolster the Manx economy. More importantly, at least in sporting terms, we were also enjoying the first wave of a massive influx of highly talented new riders. These were the first racers in a long while who would be mixing it on the greater world stage as well as at the TT, and this just had to be good news for the future. Mick Grant, Charlie Williams and Tony Rutter were, of course, all still winning at such levels, but they were being joined on the rostrums of the 1980s by up and coming stars like Joey Dunlop, Ron Haslam, Rob McElnea, Graeme Crosby, Steve Abbott, Jock Taylor, Roger Burnett, Steve Hislop and Carl Fogarty. These were very exciting times for motorcycle racing in general, and never more so than on the Island: the TT had found a new, post-GP World Championship niche and seemed more comfortable with itself, aided not least by the return of works teams from Honda, Suzuki and Yamaha.

Sadly, the tragedies continued, among competitors and fans alike, and of course the knockers dusted off all the old 'these races should be banned' arguments. Others quite rightly retaliated by quoting the often far worse statistics of how many more people were killed climbing mountains, riding horses or even crossing the road. Whatever the morality of this dispute, most enthusiasts generally accepted that all riders were competing by choice. However, some of us worried that the ever-increasing financial inducements to compete at the TT might well be tempting some riders to take needless chances at such an inherently dangerous circuit. Safety was, and still is, the major TT worry, and it was especially the case in the 1980s when the larger capacity, production-based racing machines were getting very much heavier as well as faster. This resulted in ever quicker lap times, reduced safety margins and, sadly, more than a few tragic accidents.

My profession was also greatly affected by falling lap times although not, of course, for safety reasons. Rather, it was no longer possible for us to dash around between as many differing photographic vantage points as possible, especially during the late 1980s era of Fogarty versus Hislop, as we'd done not very long before when lap times were 20 minutes and more. Lower lap times didn't just rob us of a variety of viewpoints, either. It also partly negated the considerable extra benefits we might have been enjoying from the fast focusing, wide aperture and phenomenally expensive long telephoto lenses just coming on stream, which often needed a little more time than we had to set up.

Joey Dunlop shot to fame in 1977, his second year on the Island, winning the Jubilee TT and finishing fourth in the Senior. He then won the 1980 Classic race with a record lap speed of 115.22mph – achieving this on a Yamaha so ill-prepared that he'd been obliged to hold a loose fuel tank on by his knees throughout the race. In his early days as a Honda team member, however, Joey played second fiddle to the squad's number one rider, Ron Haslam, who was being groomed for world stardom. Joey is seen here at Keppel Gate during the 1982 F1 race, again finishing second to Ron. Little did many of us guess then that "Yer Maun" would go on to win more TT races than anyone else in history.

LEFT Seven-times TT victor Mick Grant winning the 1981 Senior TT, witnessed from one of my favourite viewpoints, just behind the spectators at Ramsey Hairpin.

ABOVE Old adversaries ready for the off in the 1980 F1 race: Kiwi Graeme Crosby with a works Suzuki and Mick Grant on the works Honda. This pair were often rather too evenly matched for each other's comfort. Note the rider behind, who is not Carl Fogarty but his father George, whose crash helmet design Carl later adopted.

RIGHT A never previously seen or reported picture of the ever popular Graeme Crosby, who crashed and remounted at Signpost during the last lap of the 1981 Classic TT. This three-times winner overcooked it a bit while well in the lead, hit the bank, and pitched over the handlebars into the adjacent field, fortunately without injury. Crosby climbed back over the banking, picked the still-running bike up, continued the race to the finish – and took the win! To my considerable disappointment this typically 'Croz' incident was never reported – by the time I got back to the press room after the race, the journalists had already filed their reports and definitely had no wish to amend them. All that was noted at the time was that 'Crosby backed it off a bit on the last lap'. He didn't, and here at last is the evidence of what actually happened.

ABOVE A traditional Isle of Man view, as Mick Grant and his big Suzuki crest the Cronk-ny-Mona rise and drop down to Signpost Corner, on the way to second place behind Graeme Crosby at the 1981 Classic TT.

LEFT The Honda and Suzuki teams had an off-track spat after the 1981 F1 race, with various allegations of cheating, protests and counter-protests flying about. The race stewards finally ruled in Suzuki's favour, much to Honda's disgust, and they decided to show their displeasure by having all-new team leathers made in black overnight, and painting the works machines in funereal black too. They let their riders start the next race (including Joey Dunlop, seen here at Signpost), then drove their point home by pulling out the entire squad mid-way through the race.

RIGHT Kenny Harrison in that same 1981 Classic, blasting his lonely way through the village of Kirk Michael. But he didn't finish the race either.

ABOVE Classic winner Dennis Ireland peels off for Sulby Bridge on his RG500 Suzuki in 1982.

LEFT Ron Haslam poses with his 1982 winning works Honda F1 bike at Jurby.

ABOVE RIGHT Norman Brown burst on the scene like a breath of fresh air with a win and a second place at the 1981 Manx GP, then continued his march to fame in the 500cc World Championships. He still came back to the Island though, and is seen here at Sulby Bridge on his way to victory in the 1982 Senior TT. My view at the time was that Brown was the most complete and talented all-round road racer since Bob McIntyre and Mike Hailwood, but tragically we can never know because poor Norman was killed in a freak accident at the Silverstone Grand Prix in 1983.

RIGHT Roger Marshall at Ballacraine on the works Suzuki during the 1982 F1 race. He was an exceptionally talented rider, who could and did win anywhere – except on the Island, where the gremlins often robbed him of seemingly certain victories.

LEFT Steve Abbott and Shaun Smith with their Yamaha outfit at Kate's Cottage, during the second leg of the 1982 Sidecar race, and well on their way to finishing third. This TT-winning duo were usually in with a good chance, but the real point of this picture is the evocative setting of a much-delayed race with the sun already going down.

ABOVE Another evocative setting, the approach to Keppel Gate as it used to be back in 1982. Two great TT stalwarts, Alan Jackson and Bernard Murray, are dicing it out during the F1 race. Neither won on this occasion, but Jackson won three other TTs and Murray was a multiple Manx GP winner.

ABOVE Bernard Murray on the big F1 Kawasaki again, but a lap later, having passed Jackson and now up into fifth place.

RIGHT The wonderful Jock Taylor and passenger Benga Johansson approaching Braddan Bridge with their World Championship-winning Yamaha sidecar outfit during the 1982 races, en route to a fourth TT win while also setting a new lap record of 108.29mph. Little did we know that this would be Jock's last time on the Island, for his outfit aquaplaned at the Finnish GP a few weeks later and, though Benga survived, the jovial Scotsman was killed.

ABOVE AND LEFT Big Rob McElnea at Governor's Bridge, winning the 1983 Senior Classic TT for Suzuki. Earlier in the week Rob finished third in the F1 race, behind Joey Dunlop and Mick Grant, but having gained more experience come the final Friday, no one could get near him. He was definitely flying at Ballacrye in that first race, though!

TOP RIGHT Double winners all! Graeme McGregor on the Team George Beale 250 Yamaha, second on this occasion, at Ramsey Hairpin in the 1983 Junior .

RIGHT Dick Greasley and Stewart Atkinson at Parliament Square and well on their way to victory in that year's first Sidecar leg.

ABOVE Tony Rutter smokes off in the 1983 Senior Classic. Note the particularly good view of the soon-to-be-bulldozed old grandstand.

LEFT Manx GP winner Graham Cannell spiritedly attacks the Waterworks right-hander on the climb up the Mountain with his 250cc Yamaha during the 1983 Junior.

TOP RIGHT Steve Parrish, the former 500cc GP and truck racing star, and currently a TV commentator, surely shared the 'Jonah' badge with Roger Marshall when it came to TT racing. He even had a win taken from him after a rival team's official protest. At least here the Yamaha ace is leading triple TT winner Barry Woodland round Governor's Bridge during the 1983 Classic race.

RIGHT Keeping the marshals busy in the same race are Geoff Johnson and GP ace Simon Buckmaster: both embarrassingly dropped their bikes at near walking pace at the infamous bridge, something easily done for they had just negotiated the ultra-high-speed dash down the Mountain and probably run out of brakes. Johnson later certainly made up for his lapse by winning three TTs.

LEFT Rob McElnea on the F1 Suzuki again, but in 1984 and using all the road at the drop down to Bedstead on the way to winning a Senior and Classic TT double, with a new record lap speed for the latter of 117.13mph.

ABOVE Nick Jefferies rode a standard over-the-counter 1000cc BMW KRS roadster to eighth place in the 1984 Production race.

ABOVE LEFT Double winner Trevor Nation in fifth place on the F1 Ducati at Keppel Gate on the Mountain during the 1984 F1 race.

LEFT Three-times TT winner Geoff Johnson on his 500 Suzuki, cresting Ago's Leap just beyond the bottom of Bray Hill, in the Senior event.

ABOVE Former Manx Grand Prix winner Eddie Roberts at Governor's during the 1984 Junior race, on the unusually named Shepherd 250.

RIGHT The stylish nine-times winner Charlie Williams, nailing his 250cc Yamaha through Ramsey's Parliament Square en route to second place in the same event.

ABOVE Nine-times winner Dave Saville and passenger Dave Hall taking the left-hand bend into Braddan Bridge during the 1984 races on their 350cc Sabre outfit.

LEFT Soloists Mark Salle and Phil Nicholls emerge into the sunlight from Braddan's final right-hander on 747cc Production race Hondas in 1984. Short circuit star Salle finished sixth, but Phil wasn't placed.

TOP RIGHT Quadruple winners Trevor Ireson and Donnie Williams, seen here at Quarter Bridge with a 750 Yamaha sidecar outfit, were also not placed.

RIGHT Double winners Lowry Burton and Pat Cushnahan managed fifth and second places respectively in the two 1984 races.

LEFT Eddie Roberts on his 750cc Yamaha just before Sarah's Cottage en route to the Laurel Bank section during the 1984 Classic TT race. Closing up behind him is a young, up and coming Roger Burnett, mounted on a Sports Motorcycles 747cc Ducati/Cagiva. Although neither of them pulled up many trees on that occasion, Roger would go on to win a Senior TT in 1986 and become a works Honda GP star.

ABOVE Asger Neilsen and Ole Moller of Germany swoop through the trees with their 750cc Yamaha outfit on the short, semi-straight section between Quarter Bridge and Braddan Bridge.

LEFT Colin Bevan (248cc Yamaha) and Alan Dugdale (250cc Suzuki) race through the Laurel Bank section during the 1984 Production class race.

ABOVE Joey Dunlop, a 26-times TT winner, is seen here at Braddan Bridge, late on in the 1984 F1 race – look at the flies on his front number plate – en route to one of his many lap records.

RIGHT Joey elected to use one of Honda's easier to ride three-cylinder NS500 works GP team bikes in the Senior in 1984, and again put in the fastest lap, but sadly the bike failed to go the distance.

ABOVE Joey Dunlop seemed to hit a new – and untouchable – high with the 1987 Rothmans Hondas, as seen here at Ginger Hall, winning the F1 race with new race and lap records. He also won the Senior event that year.

LEFT Honda team supremo Barry Symmons congratulates Joey on his 1986 F1 win.

RIGHT Although the Honda team lost their cigarette sponsorship money for 1988 it made little difference to Dunlop, who just kept on winning, on the F1 Honda at Parliament Square (top), where he again took race and lap records, and with the Senior bike (right) at Ramsey Hairpin.

LEFT Ray Hanna looking neat and stylish through the ever menacing walls of Ballacraine during the 1986 Junior.

BELOW Until this Governor's Bridge moment double TT winner Gary Padgett had been leading the 1985 Lightweight Production race. At least he managed to remount and still finish third.

RIGHT This is what the TT is all about – sunshine and happy fans in close proximity to bikes racing through towns and along streets. Sidecar lads Craig McComb and Paschal Brady are just coming into Ramsey town centre during the 1985 races.

TOP Steve Parrish diving into Governor's Bridge dip on his very standard-looking FJ1100 Yamaha during a Production race in the mid-1980s.

ABOVE The ever efficient volunteer TT marshals going to work on another FJ1100 as it crashes at Ballacraine, fortunately with rider unhurt.

RIGHT Neil Tuxworth and Ray Swann are seen at Ballaugh Bridge, and looking in fine style during the 1986 F2 race. Neil, who went on to become Honda's World Superbike team boss, was on a 350 Yamaha; Ray is riding a 595cc P&M Kawasaki.

More Ballaugh shots, but this time showing Mick Chatterton racing through the village after the bridge (left), while four-times winner Dave Leach (above) literally leaps his Padgett Yamaha motocross style during the 1987 Senior.

Double TT winners Iain Duffus (above) with his Yamaha's wheels well off the deck over Rhencullen's bumps during the 1987 Production B race, and (right) Irish World Championship runner-up Eddie Laycock on a 250cc EMC, blasting through Kirk Michael village en route to Junior TT victory in the same year.

ABOVE LEFT Roger Hurst crests Sulby Bridge, whereas Des Barry (left) is about to be mopped up by Steve Linsdell on the previous corner. All of them are riding in the 1987 F1 race on 750cc Yamahas.

TOP Also during that 1987 F1 race, but at the end of the infamous Sulby Straight, and just peeling off for the right-hander, are John Caffrey (750 Yamaha) and TT veteran Alex George (Suzuki).

ABOVE The 1987 Junior TT start line and new grandstand, though the revised pit area still looks much the same.

TOP Master and pupil? Roger Marshall's former mechanic Roger Burnett leads him round Ramsey Hairpin during the 1988 Senior. Burnett had won the 1986 Senior, but the often unlucky Marshall never bettered second.

LEFT We shall spare this 1988 Production race newcomer's blushes and not name him, but note he is wearing the compulsory orange bib warning other riders he is not very experienced and this is his first TT week. As if to acknowledge the fact, our man has just clouted the Creg-ny-Baa banking, but luckily got away with it this time!

RIGHT Double TT winner Steve Cull on a 1000cc Yamaha at Ramsey Hairpin, on his record-smashing Senior lap of 119.08mph in 1988 – and then his bike's engine expired.

BELOW Nine-times winners and genuine TT heroes Mick Boddice and Chas Birks with a 750cc Ireson Yamaha at Governor's Bridge, on their way to a double victory in the 1988 races.

OVERLEAF Alan Batson in glorious sunshine, in seemingly perfect conditions, and on his way to third place with his FZ1000 Yamaha at Creg-ny-Baa during 1989's tragic 1300 Production TT. These machines, of up to 1300cc capacity, had to be fitted with standard road tyres and during the race two of the TT's finest riders, Phil Mellor and Steve Henshaw, lost tyre traction at phenomenal speeds. Both were killed.

ABOVE Carl Fogarty on the F1 start line with his RC 30 Honda. It was a bit of a mixed bag of a year for Carl, with fourth places in this race and the Junior TT (top), third in the 125cc Ultra Lightweight and just one win, in the 750 Production TT class.

RIGHT Ian Jones in the pits to refuel his 1989 Senior 888 Ducati.

LEFT Jamie Whitham scored a third place in the new 1989 Supersport 600 class race, and is seen here at Creg-ny-Baa with the works Heron Suzuki GB-entered 750 on his way to sixth berth in the F1 class.

ABOVE Whitham's team-mate, the ever popular family man and triple TT winner Phil 'Mez' Mellor, rounding Ramsey Hairpin for the last time on the too fast, under-tyred and generally massive 1300cc Production Suzuki before losing control in a fatal crash at Ballig.

RIGHT The impromptu tribute from the fans to 'Mez', on the evening after the race, replaced now by a brass plaque in his memory.

LEFT Barry Woodland rounds Ramsey Hairpin on the works-entered Yamaha 1000 FZR in the fatal 1989 1300 Production TT. Top rider Barry finished twelfth that day, but won three TTs before his so-promising career was ended by terrible injuries suffered when he was involved in a head-on TT circuit crash while he was practising unofficially when the roads were still open.

ABOVE Works Kawasaki ace Ray Swann sets off on the 750 in that same year's F1 race with those other great TT stalwarts, Ian Young (46), Kenny Harrison (49) and Bob Jackson (53). Later on in the same race (right) Ray is shadowing Howard Selby (Yamaha OW01) at Signpost.

TOP LEFT This 1989 Senior TT rider gets his pit signals.

BELOW LEFT Phil Nicholls is seen from behind on the F1 Honda at Bedstead. A rural view then, but changed forever as the course at this point now runs between two housing estates.

ABOVE Dave Leach won four TTs, including 1989's ill-fated 1300 Production race, and is seen here on his Yamaha starting the Mountain climb between Whitegates and Stella Maris in Ramsey.

RIGHT Steve Henshaw, another of my old friends, who died doing what he loved best during that same fateful 1300 Production race. He was killed at Quarry Bends when his road tyre-equipped Yamaha left the track a few minutes after this picture was taken.

OVERLEAF On a happier note, Johnny Rea, father of the modern-day British Superbike Championship racer Jonathan, at Waterworks on his 250cc Yamaha, winning the 1989 Junior, his only TT win.

1990s

NEW HORIZONS

If the 1980s were great times for the TT races then it must be argued the 1990s were even better, the decade kicking off with the fabulous Steve Hislop versus Carl Fogarty rivalry. Both were in such record-breaking form that neither seemed catchable – except by the other! Fogarty's fantastic 1992 Senior TT lap record of 123.61mph, for instance, stood for another six years, yet it was Hislop who won that race on the unfancied Wankel-engined Norton, and scored the first (and last!) all-British victory in that prestigious event since way back in the very early 1960s.

Such was the Herculean rivalry between these two that it was probably safer for both when Fogarty eventually moved over to World Superbike racing. TT fans hardly lost out, though, as the impressive Phillip McCallen instantly filled his spot, and the great Joey Dunlop was, of course, still in the wings. Joey seemed to have lost form on the big bikes following a massive crash on the mainland at Brands Hatch and, apart from the 1995 Senior, would not win another large machine-capacity TT race during this decade, but he did make this era's lightweight races almost his own. Jim Moodie was also coming to the fore, as were Ian Simpson, Michael Rutter, John McGuinness, Ian Lougher, Adrian Archibald, and the late great David Jefferies. In the sidecar class Mick Boddice, Rob Fisher and Dave Molyneux, with their various different passengers, mostly reined supreme.

The roaring 90s also witnessed a lot of major programme changes. Some worked very well, like the traditional two-stroke engine-based Junior TT changing to a race for Production machine-based 600cc four-strokes, but the single cylinder machine racing class, introduced in 1994, was a lot less well supported and proved rather short lived. The races for 750 to 1010cc Production machines from 1996 onwards proved very much more popular, but the massive changes made during the following season to the Senior were an unmitigated disaster. No-one could know in advance who would be riding or, for that matter, on what, so the Senior page in the official race programme was left as a blank! This virtually destroyed any interest in what should have been the biggest race, and continued to cost the TT series dearly for several more years: many fans either chose to go home early or, even worse, they simply decided not to visit the Island at all, as did many of the media.

On the photographic front, however, things were still improving. Autofocusing (AF) began appearing on professional cameras during 1989, although this facility, at least in my view, remains something of a dubious asset. Indeed, it could be likened to having Valentino Rossi or Michael Schumacher standing by to work things, but not letting them do the riding or driving!

On his first visit to the Island in 1988, Phil McCallen scored a unique double by winning both the Manx Grand Prix Lightweight Newcomers and the Lightweight races. After switching to the TT proper for the 1990s he was given a works ride by Honda, snapped up as the fastest new kid on the block. By 1993 he was tipped by arch-rival Steve Hislop as being the rider most likely to blow himself and Joey Dunlop into the weeds. But in the F1 race Phil could not better second behind to his popular Honda team-mate Nick Jefferies, who scored his only TT win. The hotly tipped McCallen then suffered nearly a week of mechanical retirements before things finally came right with a very convincing win in Friday's Senior. He went on to all-time TT greatness with a final total of 11 victories.

LEFT This is a super bit of road between Greeba Bridge and Ballacraine, although in bright sunlight the strong shadows cast by the trees can pose some very real problems, as no doubt here for aces Eddy Wright and Steve Campbell, who finished sixth in both 1990 Sidecar TT races.

ABOVE Malcolm Wheeler and Derek Chatterton on 250cc Kawasakis, and climbing the Mountain during the 1990 Supersport 400 race. Malcolm missed victory in the 1986 Production Class C race by just one second, which to this day is the closest margin in history.

RIGHT Following a long family tradition, Roy and Tom Hanks with an Ireson 350cc outfit, just passing Kate's Cottage, and in fifth place in this 1990 Sidecar race B.

LEFT Wet, wet, wet. Dean Ashton and Rory Thomson passing between the numerous dangers of Kirk Michael village on matching FZR600 Yamahas during the 1990 Supersport 600 race, won by Brian Reid.

ABOVE Barry Woodland leaving Quarter Bridge on the Team Loctite 400 Yamaha in the same year's Supersport 400 TT. He finished eighth.

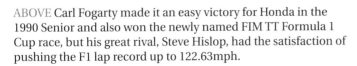

ABOVE Carl Fogarty made it an easy victory for Honda in the 1990 Senior and also won the newly named FIM TT Formula 1 Cup race, but his great rival, Steve Hislop, had the satisfaction of pushing the F1 lap record up to 122.63mph.

RIGHT Fogarty's last TT week, in 1992, before quoting safety reasons for withdrawing. He's seen here at Ballacraine on the works Yamaha, and on course for an easy victory in the F1 race until his gearbox broke on the fifth lap. Later that week Steve Hislop won the Senior on the budget-priced Norton, with Fogarty taking second place. In trying to stay with Steve, however, Carl put in a staggeringly fast lap of 123.61mph, a new lap record that would stand for the next six years.

OVERLEAF The 1990 Supersport 400 TT, one of the finest and closest-fought races ever. Carl Fogarty (Honda), Steve Cull (Kawasaki), Nick Jefferies and Dave Leach (both Yamaha) are dicing nearly neck and neck with each other as they enter Ramsey: the proverbial blanket could have been thrown over them! This is how it stayed for much of the race, though Steve Cull eventually dropped back to be replaced under the blanket by Steve Ward. Leach eventually took the victory from Fogarty, Ward, Jefferies, Brian Reid and Steve Hislop. Amazingly, just 22.4 seconds separated the first five.

LEFT Ginger Hall, an ever popular viewing spot, not least because of the refreshment and toilet facilities in the pub! Spectators can also park in the side road, then move off again between laps (or races) to Sulby Cross Roads, or use the back roads to go right over the Mountain to the Bungalow for a change of viewpoint. The outfit seen here is crewed by Richard Crossley and Catherine Jenkins.

ABOVE Mark Westmoreland nailing his 1991 Junior TT 250cc Yamaha at the ultra-fast blind left-hand bend called Barregarrow Top, which lies on the hilltop where the B10 road to Sartfield crosses the TT course. Although it does not come over in the picture, take my word for it that this is *the* most frightening place to watch from, especially from the banking on the inside of the course.

RIGHT 'The one who has the most toys wins', or so it says on Tom Bennett and Doug Jewell's 600cc Suzuki outfit for the 1991 races. Just look at the close proximity of those Ramsey shop walls, houses and sandbags, all illustrating rather well that the TT circuit has absolutely no margin for error.

ABOVE Photographers very rarely get to the frighteningly fast Cronk-ny-Mona section, seen here during the 1991 Senior. Just look at the spectator proximity – many people, including children, are just lying on the grass, without so much as a crash barrier in sight.

LEFT Another rarely pictured corner is Bedstead, a couple of hundred yards up from Governor's Bridge, and by the looks of it Dave Woolams will very shortly be pitting his 1991 Ducati F1 bike to fix that broken fairing, which can be seen flapping dangerously free in the breeze.

RIGHT The reverse view of Barregarrow Top at the moment the fully committed rider has to aim his or her bike down the Big Dipper and plunge to Barregarrow Bottom, an equally frightening spot.

LEFT Eddy Wright and Andy Hetherington racing towards Parliament Square in Ramsey with their 350cc Shellbourne sidecar outfit, to take fourth place on a truly gorgeous day in 1991.

RIGHT David Morris drops down into Governor's Bridge, in totally different conditions, during the 1990 Senior. Note the marshal standing by the wall on the right and attempting to look inconspicuous, with the blackboard, which accompanies a black flag. He is waiting to 'black-flag' or warn the rider whose number is chalked on the board that they *must* stop at the pits. Other marshals, further back up the course, will have radioed that they have either spotted an infringement, or something dangerously wrong with the bike of which the unsuspecting rider will not yet be aware. Three-times TT winner Morris, meanwhile, can carry on with his race as the chalked-up number is not his.

BELOW Dave Morris again, entering the first part of Braddan Bridge during the 1991 Supersport 600 race.

LEFT Five-times TT winner Brian Reid on his 250cc Yamaha at Keppel Gate in 1990 (above left), a wonderful spot to watch from in good weather, but thoroughly miserable if the day turns wet or cold. Brian failed to finish that race, but is seen again (left) on the Yamaha FZR in the same year's exciting Supersport 400 race at the Gooseneck. He was chasing Dave Leach, Carl Fogarty, Steve Ward and Nick Jefferies for an eventual fifth place.

ABOVE Phillip McCallen at Brandywell with his works 250cc Honda, en route to sixth place in the 1990 Junior race. This was not one of his better performances, but Phil would later become the dominant force in TT racing, winning no less than 11 times before injuries prematurely ended his phenomenal career.

RIGHT One of my favourite pictures: this is Cronk-ny-Mona just after the right-hander at Hillberry, and double winner Brian Morrison is riding his 750cc Loctite Yamaha flat to the stop but still accelerating on his way to third in the 1991 F1 race.

LEFT Steve Hislop and Carl Fogarty were Honda team-mates in 1991. Both were so focused at the time that no other rider could match them, including fellow factory men Joey Dunlop and Phillip McCallen. Hislop unofficially raised the lap record in practice to a staggering 124.36mph, and come the all-important F1 race he requested a higher start number than his rival, going off at number 11 to Fogarty's number 8, and then setting a new course record from a standing start. He upped the pace again, to a record 123.48 mph and, with Carl's machine stuttering, Hislop caught him on the road, in essence rubbing it in to his main rival that he was already a beaten man. The next day Fogarty flew out to the States for a World Superbike race, leaving Joey Dunlop to ride his machine to second in the Senior, with Hislop taking an easy victory.

ABOVE The talented duo came together again in 1992. Fogarty had switched allegiance from Honda to Yamaha, while Hislop had no works ride at all until a couple of weeks before the TT, when Honda's ex-team boss, Barry Symmons, asked if Steve would consider riding a British Norton for next to nothing. The rest is history. Hislop very nearly won the opening F1 race with the rotary engined machine, but lost out via a necessary long pit stop while mechanics ripped off part of the bike's fairing to counter serious engine overheating. This dropped Steve to second place behind Phil McCallen, after Fogarty's machine also struck trouble. Come the Senior race on Friday, however, literally no-one else counted. It was a case of unfinished business between Hislop and Fogarty as the fastest Senior TT in history unfolded, with Hislop on the shoestring budget Norton, here at Creg-ny-Baa, winning this David verses Goliath grudge match at a phenomenal race average of 121.28mph. What mattered most to the 40,000 ecstatic fans, apart from having just witnessed a truly wonderful race, was that this was also the first Senior TT win by a British bike since 1961, when Mike Hailwood also won on a Norton. There was hardly a dry eye on the Island, for we all knew it could not happen again: the tiny little Norton company was already technically bankrupt.

LEFT Riding for Honda again, Steve Hislop blasts away from the start line on his way to victory in the 1994 F1 race, and (above) moments earlier getting the 'one minute to go' board with Steve Ward (2), Joey Dunlop and the rest.

RIGHT It was a magical moment when Hislop was presented with the historic Senior TT trophy in 1992, having won on the Norton from Carl Fogarty (Yamaha, left) and Robert Dunlop (right) who also rode a Norton.

ABOVE Iain Duffus on the FZR Yamaha sneaking inside Simon Beck's 600cc Honda at the Gooseneck, on his way to winning the 1994 Supersport 600 TT. During a highly promising career Beck won the Ulster Grand Prix and the Senior Manx but never a TT. Sadly, he was killed during practice for the 1999 F1 race.

LEFT Double winner Duffus again, but this time climbing the Mountain on the 1992 750cc F1 Kawasaki, and just about skimming the very solid stone wall he had been heading straight for a few moments earlier.

RIGHT Robert Holden (Yamaha OW01) and Steve Ward (750 Honda), neck and neck at Creg-ny-Baa with no quarter being given as they belt down the Mountain during the 1992 Senior race. Singles TT winner Holden was another rider who lost his life racing in the Island, during practice in 1996.

Two lonesome studies of six-times TT winner Ian Lougher – on the Mountain and well on his way to winning the 1990 Junior (above), and mid-way along the undulating Cronk-y-Voddy straight in the 1992 race on the TCR 250 (right), when the best he could manage was fifth.

LEFT Steve Hazlett at the Waterworks, climbing the Mountain with his Honda RC30 in the 1992 F1, another racer who gave his all doing what he loved.

ABOVE Kiwi Shaun Harris racing the ugly but effective Britten 1000cc V-twin through Kirk Michael village during the 1993 Senior.

RIGHT In 1993 Manxmen Dave Molyneux and Karl Ellison, seen here at Sulby Bridge, did the double. This duo has won the Sidecar class an amazing 11 times.

The great Jim Moodie could never be ruled out of TT contention, whatever he was riding. The eight-times winner is seen (left) riding the backside off an unfancied 600cc Honda while heading Rory Thomson at the Gooseneck and en route to sixth place in the 1990 Supersport 600 race, and (above) again in equally aggressive motocross style at Ballaugh Bridge, this time winning the 1993 Supersport 400 class with a race average of 111.43mph.

TOP Jim Moodie at Braddan Bridge on an FZR Yamaha and winning the 1994 Supersport 400 race, and at Ramsey winning the 1996 Singles TT (above).

RIGHT Nick Jefferies on the 1000cc Britten V-Twin, taking Ago's Leap flat out during the 1994 Senior. All-rounder Nick sadly only won a TT once – the F1 in 1993 – but he was very rarely off the leaderboard in dozens of other races.

LEFT The great Joey Dunlop was a man of superstitions, and while everyone else would have been ready on the grid, Joey could usually be seen walking around on the sidelines in his socks, prior to the running-late ritual of always putting his left boot on first!

ABOVE Honda team-mates Steve Hislop and Joey Dunlop take the 1991 Senior TT finishing flag virtually neck and neck, though Hislop would win by virtue of having started well behind Joey, who always preferred starting and riding as number three.

RIGHT How they finished: (left to right) Dunlop (second), winner Hislop and Phillip McCallen (third), all on works Hondas.

TOP LEFT The master at work! Joey Dunlop on his 1995 250cc Honda, slipping inside Kent Lund at Ramsey Hairpin while winning the Lightweight race at 115.68mph, when he also achieved a new 250 fastest lap speed of 117.57 mph.

LEFT Joey entering Kirk Michael during the 1993 F1 race.

ABOVE Dunlop is on the grid with manager Davy Wood, getting ready for the 1994 F1 race where, as ever Honda-mounted, he finished third.

RIGHT The following year, 1995, at Quarter Bridge and winning the Senior at an average speed of 119.11mph.

OVERLEAF Joey Dunlop at Ballacraine during the 1996 Senior TT, seen lying second and some way behind team-mate Phillip McCallen. Joey won both the Lightweight and Ultra Lightweight races that year, but finished a fairly lowly seventh in the F1 event, a race again won by McCallen.

ABOVE Emerging from Governor's Bridge dip, Joey Dunlop and Phillip McCallen with their Senior TT works Hondas in 1996, about to finish first and second, with Phil doing the winning by virtue of his later start number.

LEFT Joey Dunlop leaves Parliament Square, Ramsey, in the same race.

RIGHT Dunlop besting Chris Heath (1) but not up and coming Adrian Archibald (13) during the new 600cc capacity Junior race in 1999. Archibald finished fourth, Joey fifth.

Simon Beck (left) jumps Ballaugh Bridge in fine style while in third place on the Team Rumi 701 before retiring in the new for 1994 Singles race, and (above) Kawasaki-mounted David Goodley at the Nook in the F1 that same year.

ABOVE Senior Manx Grand Prix winner Alan Bennallick aviates his Honda RC30 at Ago's Leap during the 1994 Senior TT.

RIGHT TT stalwart Steve Sinnott with Dave Corlett and their 600cc Yamaha outfit racing into Parliament Square in the 1994 Sidecar class.

TOP LEFT Privateer Nigel Davies leading the 1994 F1 race by a handsome margin at Ramsey Hairpin and revelling in the truly appalling conditions that narrowed the considerable speed gap between the likes of his over-the-counter machine and the rival works bikes. This race was actually stopped mid-distance due to the bad weather, and many of us thought the final verdict should have been his. Instead, the powers that be decided on a rerun next day, which Steve Hislop won on his works Honda in perfect conditions. Davies, a Senior Manx GP winner in 1993, finished sixth, unable to match the speed of the top machines in the dry.

LEFT Nigel Davies rounding Signpost, and well on his way to second place in the 1998 Production TT on his 750cc Kawasaki ZX9RR.

ABOVE Ashley Law (Honda) and Simon Smith (Kawasaki) have a bit of a coming-together at Ramsey Hairpin during the 1995 Junior race, though luckily neither fell off.

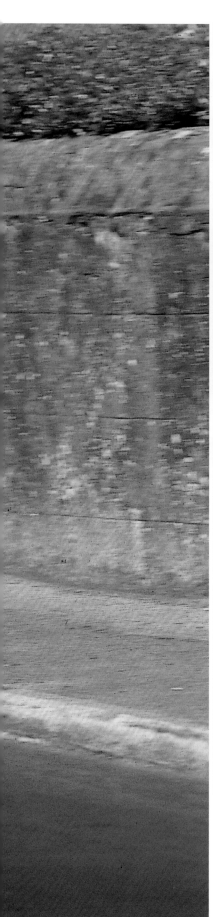

LEFT Sandra Barnett and her CBR 600 Honda at the frighteningly fast Whitegates section during the 1995 Junior race. A trials rider and all-round competitor, Sandra contested most solo classes and was for a long time the fastest, and best, lady rider in the Island. Indeed, she was a top-line competitor on sheer merit, setting the fastest lap by a lady rider of 114.87mph in the 1997 Junior.

ABOVE Double winner Geoff Bell with passenger Nick Roche and their Windle outfit, climbing May Hill in Ramsey in 1995 and well on their way to third and fifth places in the two Sidecar races.

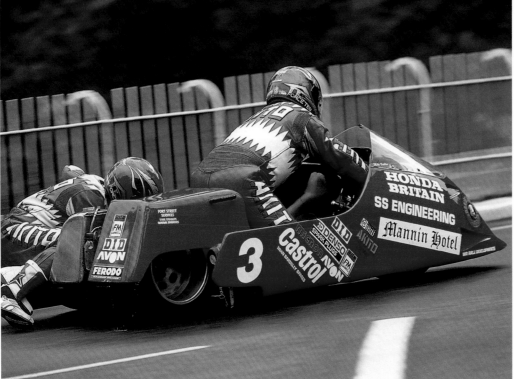

ABOVE Bob Heath was one of the Island's greatest and most enthusiastic exponents, winning no fewer than 11 Manx GPs as well as top-ten TT placings. Here he's at Ramsey Hairpin, in the 1995 Singles race, finishing fourth on the BMR Seeley.

LEFT Not one of the better years for nine-times winner Mick Boddice, seen here at Braddan Bridge in 1996 with passenger Dave Wells on the Ireson Honda: they were fifth in the first Sidecar race and rare non-finishers in the second.

RIGHT Manxmen Artie Oates and passenger Greg Mahon aim their Yamaha outfit between the stone walls and telegraph poles through Whitegates on the climb out of Ramsey during the 1995 races.

LEFT Ducks away! Mike Casey going for the gap in the middle on his Junior Honda as mother duck shepherds her offspring across the TT course near Ballacraine, heading for the nearest stream. You could actually set your watch by her that week for this was a daily occurrence, and they always (at least as far I know) made it safely across. Quite a few riders almost had chickens, though!

ABOVE Double winner Shaun Harris looking very focused on the Suzuki GSX-R at Parliament Square in Ramsey during the 1996 Production TT.

Veteran Ian Lougher shot to fame in the 1983 Manx Grand Prix before going on to score six TT
wins, including winning the 1997 Ultra Lightweight race on a 125cc Honda, as seen (above) on the
Mountain, and during the 1996 F1 race at Brandywell (right), heading Alan Bennallick.

TOP LEFT Michael Rutter (Ducati) leads the works Hondas of Nick Jefferies and Phil McCallen on the Mountain road approaching Keppel Gate during the 1996 F1 race, in which this talented trio finished 1–2–3 in the reverse order. McCallen was nearly untouchable that year. He won four races and took four fastest laps, though without challenging Carl Fogarty's long-standing record.

LEFT Rutter was Honda mounted for 1997 and is seen here at the Gooseneck, and in second place to team-mate Phil McCallen, in the F1 race.

ABOVE Always fully focused, Phil McCallen uses every inch of the road while winning three races in 1997. He certainly gave the likes of Allan 'Grandad' Warner quite a shock when he lapped him during the F1 race at the Gooseneck – Allan was so surprised he very nearly fell off!

Eleven-times winner Phil McCallen at Signpost, winning the 1997 Production TT on a Honda CBR 900 FireBlade (above), and chasing Nick Jefferies at Bedstead, en route to winning the same class on a similar bike in 1996 (right). It was such a shame that this brilliant rider's career ended on doctors' orders after a serious crash at another circuit.

ABOVE A gaggle of riders and one lone spectator at Hailwood Rise on the Mountain in superb weather during the 1997 Junior. The race was won by Ian Simpson from Phil McCallen.

LEFT Roy Hanks and Phil Biggs approach Governor's Bridge with their Ireson NRH outfit to win the 1997 Sidecar race A.

RIGHT The same year, at the same place, ten-times TT winner Rob Fisher and his passenger Rick Long win race B with the Baker/Express outfit, and with the best lap speed of 110.45mph.

ABOVE Started in the 1970s, the parade lap for past masters had become a wonderfully evocative event by 1997. Derek Minter, seen here nearest the camera on a 500cc Norton, was the very first man to lap the Island at over 100mph on a similar single cylinder machine back in the 1960s.

RIGHT Three-times TT winner Adrian Archibald (above right) on the Sanyo works Honda VTR 1000 at the Gooseneck during the 1997 F1 race, and the ever-consistent Steve Linsdell (right) with the unusual leading link front fork Flitwick 750 cc Yamaha at Ballacraine in the same race.

LEFT Tim Leech leads Simon Smith up Hailwood Heights from the Bungalow on a gorgeous day in 1997 during a between-races practice session.

ABOVE Richard 'Milky' Quayle guns his Production CBR 900 Honda through the same section. Richard was one of the best home-brewed Manx riders ever, and won three Manx Grand Prix races and a Lightweight TT before a serious accident ended his riding career. Happily he is now very much involved with TT race organisation.

Ian Simpson blasts off the 1996 Senior TT start line on the works-backed V&M Honda RC45 (above), and at Brandywell in the same year's F1 race (right). Never the luckiest TT rider, Ian was always one of the hardest to beat, certainly deserving more than his three wins. Sadly, gremlins so often intervened.

LEFT Anita Buxton on a Honda FireBlade and about to be scooped up by Yamaha-mounted John Crellin on the approach to Signpost during the 1998 Production race.

RIGHT Ian Simpson at the Gooseneck on his way to fourth place on the V&M Honda RC45 in the 1997 F1 race.

BELOW Simpson at Ballacraine on the works Honda, winning the 1998 F1 race with a fastest lap of 123.28mph.

TOP LEFT Jason Griffiths, son of 1960s TT star Selwyn, on his way to Union Mills and gunning his 1998 F1 Honda to fifth. He repeated that placing in the Senior after a much-troubled practice week, including having to pull in at Ballacraine (left) for adjustments.

ABOVE Often overshadowed by older brother Joey, this is Robert Dunlop just leaving Braddan Bridge and well on his way to winning the 1998 Ultra Lightweight race on a 125cc Honda at 106.38mph. Robert was a five-times TT winner.

ABOVE Gary Dynes, just leaving Ballaugh village for fifth place on his 125cc Honda during the 1998 Ultra Lightweight race.

RIGHT Terry McGinty, also in fifth place, but on a Harris Suzuki in the same year's Singles TT – and having very nearly clouted the wall at Braddan Bridge.

John McGuinness traversing the Mountain with his 125cc Aprilia during the 1997 Ultra Lightweight race (left), and a couple of years later, passing through Ramsey's Parliament Square, winning the 1999 Lightweight at 116.79mph on his Vimto 250cc Honda (above).

ABOVE Current top star and 11-times TT winner John McGuinness on his way to a very wet third place at Ramsey Hairpin on the 250cc Vimto Honda during the 1998 Lightweight race.

RIGHT Way back in 1996, one of the new kids on the block, and running a long way behind the top men during the 1996 Lightweight TT, McGuinness is seen in this rear view leading Alan 'Bud' Jackson over Ballaugh Bridge.

LEFT Another new kid on the block in 1996 was number 27, David Jefferies, setting off on a standard roadster-looking Honda in the Senior race and and watched by his proud father Tony (in the wheelchair), himself a triple TT winner. Little did we know then that this great Yorkshire motorcycling dynasty was about to introduce us to another all-time TT great.

ABOVE Three years on and the seemingly unbeatable David Jefferies is at Sulby Bridge, winning the F1 race with the fastest lap of 123.26mph. He also won the Senior and Production races that year to make it three in a week.

One of the biggest changes for 2000 was the need for a new Clerk of the Course, as the brilliant J. J. 'Jacky' Woods decided now was a good time to stand down. Everyone missed his undoubted great wisdom, but it was all systems go again with 721 riders entered from 20 different countries.

On paper, at least, David Jefferies and Adrian Archibald were the favourites for the first races of the new millennium, though no-one would ever rule out young William Joseph Dunlop, even aged 48. Joey was a TT-winning institution. Arguably, what followed was one of the most unpredictable and best of TT weeks since the era of Hailwood or Fogarty. Most of us had expected Jefferies to win everything – and instead he found himself slugging it out every inch of the way against a back-on-form Joey Dunlop. This surprise battle of the titans ended with three wins apiece, as Jefferies upped the fastest ever lap time to 125.69mph in the Senior, and Dunlop won the Formula 1 race again after a lapse of 12 years. Although John McGuinness at least went home with the TT Singles trophy, the expected challenge from Adrian Archibald faded.

Sadly, within months the great Joey Dunlop was dead, killed while competing in a relatively meaningless race in Estonia and leaving many, including myself, wondering if the TT even had a future without him. The following year the TT races were cancelled, due to foot and mouth disease on the mainland, and after that enforced break – and a full year of mourning – it then seemed okay to continue without Joey.

And what a year 2002 was, with the Island festooned in welcome-back banners, and that man David Jefferies carrying on from where he left off, with three more race wins and three race and lap records smashed. It was not entirely a walkover, though, as Ian Lougher also won two races, with both Bruce Anstey and Richard Quayle winning one apiece and, in the Sidecar class, Rob Fisher and passenger Rick Long totally dominating to conclude a particularly brilliant week.

Everything seemed at least as promising come 2003, with many pundits predicting the great David 'DJ' Jefferies might even manage the first ever 130mph lap. It all went terribly wrong, however, when Jefferies's big Suzuki reputedly hit a patch of oil while he was riding it flat out through Crosby village in practice. David was tragically killed in a horror scenario with the Suzuki demolishing a stone wall and bringing down a telegraph pole, leaving Jim Moodie, who was behind him, enmeshed in the wreckage and badly injured. The accident caused many, including myself, to question if these ever faster and more dangerous races deserved a future.

After much thought I did go back the following year, not least to find out if I still felt the same and, as always, the racing in 2004 was fantastic. Although I will never say a harsh word against my beloved TT I have not been back since, but do wish god speed (safely!) to those who do continue to go, in whatever role they play.

David Jefferies set the second fastest TT lap ever, at 124.43mph, during practice for the first race of the new millennium. Then, perhaps unwisely, he stated he could have gone much faster and might smash the all-time record in the race itself, though his Yamaha R1's engine had other ideas, blowing itself to pieces at Ballig. Jefferies tackled the rest of that TT week with a vengeance, ending Honda's five-year domination by easily winning the Junior race with a 600cc R6 for Yamaha (here at May Hill), the 600 Production race and the Senior. The spoils were divided between the new boy and the old master. Were that, and the new 121.15mph Junior record lap not enough, Jefferies led the Senior TT throughout, with his 1000cc V&M sponsored Yamaha R1, winning by over 40 seconds from his team-mate Michael Rutter. He also shattered the previously unattainable 125mph barrier with a phenomenal 125.69mph lap record.

ABOVE LEFT Michael Rutter at Whitegates, and in fifth place on the V&M 600cc Yamaha during the 2000 Junior race.

LEFT Denis McCullough in second place in the Ultra Lightweight race on the Lunney 125cc Honda, ahead of Darran Lindsay in fifth on another Honda, but 16.1 seconds behind 2000 winner Joey Dunlop.

ABOVE Shaun Harris of New Zealand riding in that year's Production class for Suzuki in absolutely awful conditions. No wonder Shaun almost tiptoed around Quarter Bridge! He later won two Production TT races, in 2003.

Another wet race day for six-times winner Ian Lougher in 2000, as he carefully follows the white line out of Ramsey Hairpin with his Yamaha R1, en route to fourth place in the F1 race (above), and two years later with the TAS 1000 Suzuki, running neck and neck in fourth place with Paul Owen (Yamaha R1) at Stella Maris (right).

LEFT Joey Dunlop certainly reminded everyone he was still around come the millennium TT week, with an F1 race win, as seen here at Ramsey Hairpin.

RIGHT Dunlop also scooped wins in the Lightweight and Ultra Lightweight races in 2000. He heads Darran Lindsay in the latter, both of them on 125cc Hondas, passing through Parliament Square on the way to his 26th TT victory.

BELOW Seen here at May Hill, Joey also took fourth place on a 600cc Honda in the 2000 Junior race. Sadly, a couple of months later, the seemingly immortal Dunlop went off to contest an unimportant race in Estonia as a favour for a friend, and tragically lost his life far from home after his favourite 125cc Honda aquaplaned on surface water in awful race conditions, causing him to hit a trackside tree. We shall not see his likes again.

ABOVE Ten-times winner Rob Fisher and passenger Rick Long at Signpost with their LMS Yamaha in 2002. They took a double Sidecar victory that year and demoralised the opposition with a 110.75mph average in the second race and a new fastest lap of 111.58 mph.

RIGHT Jim Moodie, eight times a winner, also at Signpost, winning the 2002 Junior TT on a 600cc Yamaha. At an average race speed of 119.22mph and with a new fastest lap of 120.63mph, this was quite an achievement for a roadster-based 600.

OVERLEAF Parliament Square in Ramsey during the 2002 Production 1000 TT. Jim Moodie is in fourth place on the colourful V&M Yamaha.

TOP LEFT David Jefferies showing a clean pair of heels with his 600cc Yamaha, racing out of Ramsey between Whitegates and Stella Maris on his way to winning the 2000 Junior TT at 119.33mph.

LEFT Jefferies at Ramsey Hairpin, winning the 2002 F1 race for Suzuki.

ABOVE David at Creg-ny-Baa in the same race, when he not only won at record speed but also pushed the all-time lap record to 126.68mph, raising it again later that week in the Senior TT to an incredible 127.49mph.

FAR LEFT We did not know it then, but the 2002 Senior was the last TT race for the brilliant David Jefferies. Seen at Quarter Bridge on the 1000cc TAS Suzuki, he is not only winning as usual but also smashing the race and lap records at 124.74 and 127.49 mph respectively, despite the less than pleasant weather.

LEFT David Jefferies on the TAS Suzuki during the first lap of Thursday's pre-TT week full afternoon practice session in 2003. Tragically he would not come round again: a truly horrific accident cost him his life at Crosby, a mere couple of minutes later.

ABOVE An impromptu memorial from fans and family to David at that fatal Crosby wall, later that same evening. This, more than any other accident, made me question my own future commitment to my beloved TT.

LEFT A rather nice view of the Manx flags and Parliament Square, Ramsey, during the 2002 Production 1000 race. The riders are Simon 'Ronnie' Smith on a Suzuki GSXR 750 and Johnny Barton with a 998 Ducati.

ABOVE Dave Molyneux with Craig Hallam and the DMR 600 Honda outfit, also in Ramsey, winning the Sidecar B race in 2003. Manxman Molyneux had won 11 TTs at the time of writing, and supposedly has now retired – but just watch this space!

LEFT Victor Gilmore from Joey Dunlop's home town of Ballymoney, keeping the flag flying for Ulster, with his 1000cc Suzuki at Parliament Square during the 2003 F1 race.

ABOVE Black-flagged! The race marshals are stopping Mick Harvey and Stephen Taylor's 600cc Shellbourne outfit, just past Schoolhouse Bend in Ramsey mid-race, during the 2003 Sidecar TT, so they can inspect the machine for safety's sake. Earlier on in the lap marshals must have spotted something worrying about the bike, like a loose fairing or exhaust pipe, and will have radioed ahead to have the outfit stopped and checked. Once any problem had been fixed this duo would have been credited with the time lost and sent on their way again.

RIGHT Richard Britton of Enniskillen with his Honda at Sulby Bridge, en route to a well-deserved second place in the 2003 Lightweight 400 race.

ABOVE LEFT Paul Dobbs at Ginger Hall on a 750cc Suzuki during the 2003 Production 1000 race, when he finished with a time just outside bronze replica standard. Look at the proximity of his head and that infamous telegraph pole! Back in Geoff Duke's day this pole stood outside the railings, and Geoff used to cock his head over to the right to avoid hitting it. A few other riders forgot to do this, so the authorities eventually decided to move the pole inside the fencing. Indeed, since this picture was taken they have also now padded the fence.

LEFT A whole gaggle of Production TT riders heading down for Brandish in 2002, on one of the fastest stretches of the course.

ABOVE Welshman Paul Owen at Ballacraine with a mere 250cc Honda against the bigger bikes during the 2003 Junior 600 TT. He rode it well, too, with 27th place out of 63, winning a bronze replica at 111.30mph.

LEFT It's not often nowadays that recent World Champions come to race in the Island, but Austrians Kl__ Klaffenböck and passenger Christian Parzer certainly bucked the trend when they came over in __94 with a 600c Yamaha sidecar outfit. They had a good first-timer go, despite a considerable lack of circuit knowledge – it wasn't a fairytale debut, but they lapped at 104.14mph before going out with mechanical problems at Glen Vine.

ABOVE Currently an 11-times TT winner, and unquestionably the man to beat, this is John McGuinness on the 400cc Honda at Signpost, close to winning the 400 Lightweight race in 2003. The following year John not only won the race again but also blitzed the F1 and Junior TTs, with fastest laps in all three races. He'd looked as though he might virtually annihilate all others in the 2004 Senior, too, after a staggering 127.19mph opening lap from the standing start was then consolidated into a 21.3s lead and a mid-race average speed of 127.02mph. Unfortunately clutch trouble forced his eventual retirement at Ramsey.

LEFT John McGuinness passing through Parliament Square on the F1 Yamaha R1, on his way to winning the 2004 race at a phenomenal average speed of 125.38mph. He also achieved a standing-start lap record of 127.68mph, smashing David Jefferies's 2002 record, believed by many to be unbeatable, by 3.2 seconds.

ABOVE Superman McGuinness in 2004 again, at Creg-ny-Baa, winning the Junior race on the 600cc Yamaha R6, and yet again rewriting the TT history books by smashing both lap and race records with speeds of 122.87mph and 120.57mph respectively.

ABOVE RAF man Gordon Blackley at Ramsey on his 2003 Honda in the F1 race. Always a top-ten runner Gordon has won two Manx Grands Prix, but so far a TT win has eluded him.

RIGHT Robert Dunlop and his 125cc Honda at Braddan Bridge, on his way to finishing in second place behind Chris Palmer in the 2004 Ultra Lightweight TT. This five-times winner then announced he had lost too many friends on this dangerous course, so we had just witnessed his last TT race on the Island.

LEFT Double Manx GP winner Ryan Farquhar jumping Ballaugh Bridge in fine style on his way to winning the 2004 Production 600 race on the Winston McAdoo Kawasaki, the first rider to win a TT on a Kawasaki for many a long year. This was also the first of Ryan's two TT wins.

ABOVE Jason Griffiths in third place with the Yamaha R1 during the 2004 Production 1000 TT, and lapping newcomer Scott Crews. Welshman Griffiths, a Manx GP winner, now lives on the Island and has scored numerous top-three TT placings, but a win has so far eluded him.

LEFT One of the few races that John McGuinness didn't win in 2004, though he is still going well here at Governor's Bridge during the Senior TT. For once the R1 Yamaha let him down, though not before he had put in the race's fastest lap of 127.19mph.

ABOVE Adrian Archibald and the works 1000cc TAS/Suzuki kicking the leaves up at Quarter Bridge while winning the 2004 Senior TT from team-mate Bruce Anstey at 123.81mph.